CityPack
New York

KATE SEKULES

Adopted New Yorker Kate Sekules writes about travel, food and fitness for many magazines, including The New Yorker, Travel & Leisure, Health & Fitness, Time Out *and* Vogue. *She is also a co-author of Fodor's* New York City, *author of the forthcoming* At Night: New York, *and a consultant on the US Mobil Travel Guides.*

AA Publishing

Page 1: the World Trade
Center

Page 2 (above): SoHo
wall art

Page 23: Prometheus, Paul
Manship, Rockefeller
Center

Written by Kate Sekules
Edited, designed and produced by AA Publishing
Maps © The Automobile Association 1996
Fold-out map:
   © RV Reise- und Verkehrsverlag Munich · Stuttgart
   © Cartography: GeoData

Distributed in the United Kingdom by AA Publishing,
Norfolk House, Priestley Road, Basingstoke, Hampshire,
RG24 9NY.

The contents of this publication are believed correct at the
time of printing. Nevertheless, the publishers cannot be
held responsible for any errors or omissions or for changes in
the details given in this guide or for the consequences of any
reliance on the information provided by the same.
Assessments of attractions, hotels, restaurants and so forth
are based upon the author's own personal experience and,
therefore, descriptions given in this guide necessarily
contain an element of subjective opinion which may not
reflect the publishers' opinion or dictate a reader's own
experiences on another occasion.
**We have tried to ensure accuracy in this guide, but things do
change and we would be grateful if readers would advise us of
any inaccuracies they may encounter.**

A CIP catalogue record for this book is available from the
British Library.
ISBN 0 7495 1177 X

Published by AA Publishing (a trading name of Automobile
Association Developments Limited, whose registered office
is Norfolk House, Priestley Road, Basingstoke, Hampshire
RG24 9NY. Registered number 1878835).

Colour separation by Daylight Colour Art Pte Ltd, Singapore
Printed and bound by Dai Nippon Printing Co. (Hong
Kong) Ltd

Contents

About this book

CityPack New York is divided into six sections to cover the six most important aspects of your visit to New York.

1. NEW YORK LIFE *(pages 5–12)*
Your personal introduction to New York by author Kate Sekules
Facts and figures
Leading characters
Big events in New York's history

2. HOW TO ORGANISE YOUR TIME *(pages 13–22)*
Make the most of New York
Four one-day itineraries
Two suggested walks
Two evening strolls
Two excursions beyond the city
Calendar of events

3. NEW YORK'S TOP 25 SIGHTS *(pages 23–48)*
Your concise guide to sightseeing
Kate Sekules's own choice, with her personal introduction to each sight
Description and history
Highlights of each attraction
Comprehensive practical information
Each sight located on the inside cover of the book

4. NEW YORK'S BEST *(pages 49–60)*
What New York is renowned for
Buildings
Views
Neighbourhoods
Museums
Galleries and Outdoor Art
Gyms

5. NEW YORK: WHERE TO... *(pages 61–86)*
The best places to eat, shop, be entertained and stay
Nine categories of restaurant
Seven categories of shop
Five categories of entertainment venue
Three categories of hotel
Price bands and booking details

6. NEW YORK TRAVEL FACTS *(pages 87–93)*
Essential information for your stay

SYMBOLS
Throughout the guide a few straightforward symbols are used to denote the following categories:

✚ map reference on the fold-out map accompanying this book (see below)

✉ address

☎ telephone number

◉ opening times

❚❚ restaurant or café on premises or nearby

🚇 nearest subway station

🚌 nearest bus route

🚋 nearest overground train station

♿ facilities for visitors with disabilities

▣ admission charge

↔ other places of interest near by

❓ tours, lectures or special events

► indicates the page where you will find a fuller description

MAPS
All map references are to the separate fold-out map accompanying this book. For example, the Chrysler Building, on Lexington Avenue, has the following information: ✚ E6 – indicating the grid squares of the fold-out map in which the Chrysler Building will be found. All entries within the Top 25 Sights section are also plotted by number (not page number) on the city-centre plan located on the inside front and back covers of this book.

PRICES
Where appropriate, an indication of the cost of an establishment is given by £ signs: £££ denotes higher prices, while £ denotes lower charges.

FLOOR NUMBERS
This book reflects the American system of floor numbering. In American-English the term 'ground floor' is replaced by the term 'first floor'. Other floors are numbered accordingly.

NEW YORK
life

NEW YORK IN FIGURES

DEMOGRAPHY
- Population New York City (NYC) 7.3 million
  (of which population Manhattan 1.5 million)
- Average prison population 18,736
- Catholic New Yorkers 43.4 per cent
- Jewish New Yorkers 10.9 per cent
- Baptists 10.7 per cent
- Arrests in 1994 89,000
- Murders in 1994 517

GEOGRAPHY
- New York City area 301 square miles
  (of which Manhattan area 22.7 square miles;
  13.4 miles long by 0.8–2.3 miles wide)
- Miles of streets 6,400
- Miles of subway track 722
- Miles of waterfront 578
- Acres of parks 26,138
- Number of skyscrapers 200
- Average annual rainfall 47.25 inches
- Average annual snowfall 29.3 inches

TOURISM
- Number of visitors in 1994 24.6 million
- Number of airport passengers 77.5 million
- Number of hotel rooms 58,651
- Number of licensed taxis 11,787
- Number of old chequered cabs 8

LEISURE
- Number of restaurants 17,000
- Number of art galleries 400
- Number of Broadway theatres 35
- Number of Off-Broadway theatres 300
- Average midtown traffic speed 5.3mph
- 1995 rent for hot dog cart at Met $316,200

Cab statistics

There is a fixed number of New York taxis, though the driver population changes constantly, cab driving being a traditional occupation of newly arrived immigrants. In 1993, 1,694 new licences were granted – though not to the 29 per cent of applicants who failed the English proficiency test. At the last count, there were 85 different nationalities among New York taxi drivers, with 60 languages spoken, but no guarantee of geographical fluency – the knowledge of Manhattan required is rudimentary.

NEW YORK PEOPLE

WOODY ALLEN

Since he has one of the world's best-known faces, it's very strange actually to see Woody, and you do see him, sooner or later. 'I can never leave,' he has said. Woody shares an unspoken pact with New Yorkers. Everyone knows not to stare at him, not at the Gramercy Tavern or Elaine's, not at a Knick's game at the Garden, not even when he's onstage Mondays playing the clarinet at Michael's Pub. The Soon Yi-gate scandals of 1993 did remarkably little to taint the love his home town lavishes on the guy who made the neurotic, hypochondriac Upper East Side *mensch* into a world wide cliché.

Woody Allen

DONNA KARAN

One of the few fashion designers to command movie-star-level recognition – at least of her name – Karan (emphasise the first syllable) came to fame well over a decade ago with a capsule collection of clothes for women over 20 based on a garment that has become the staple of every wardrobe, everywhere: The Body. Launching her 'DKNY' diffusion range widened the scope of this astute businesswoman and welded the idea of her clothes to the image of New York forever, leading some to suggest that she pay royalties to the city. See her 20-storey mural at Broadway and Houston and decide for yourself.

DONALD TRUMP

You think you've heard the end of the Donald, and then he starts up another scheme or marries another blonde. A former pet project, Trump Tower, the vulgar pink and gold block on Fifth Avenue, is pure frozen 1980s, but the 1990s are treating this highest profile wheeler dealer OK too, after a shaky start. The shaky start left him in debt to the tune of $8 billion, with $975 million of it personally guaranteed. Somehow, he came out with the Plaza Hotel (though Citicorp share the control), and his Taj Mahal gambling arena in Atlantic City; meanwhile divorcing Ivana and marrying Marla. Now he's developing Riverside South – a gargantuan tract of the Upper West Side.

New York types

Korean deli owner

It's impossible to envisage life before the Korean deli. Prices are ridiculously inflated, but it's a fair tax to pay on being able to get a banana–raisin–bran–nut muffin or a floor mop at 4AM.

Personal trainer

The gym boom is waning, as everyone journeys inwardly and does yoga and Qigong, but this hasn't affected the 2:1 trainer-to-New Yorker ratio. A trainer is mentor, guru, scourge and saviour in one, and has been custom designed for NYC.

Panhandler

It's a very sad and unavoidable fact of life in the city that you will see more homeless people than you can count. Heavy competition for hardened New Yorkers' dimes leads to some irresistibly inventive lines.

9

A Chronology

Pre-16th century	New York and the surrounding lands are populated by Native Americans
1524	Giovanni da Verrazano makes the first sighting of what is to be New York
1609	Henry Hudson sails up the Hudson seeking the North West Passage
1614	Adriaen Block names the area 'New Netherland'
1625	'Niew Amsterdam' is founded by the Dutch West India Company
1626	That colony's leader, Peter Minuit, buys Manhattan Island from the Indians for $24-worth of trinkets
1664	'Wall Street's' wall fails to deter the British, who invade and rename the island 'New York', after Charles II's brother, James, the Duke of York
1763	Treaty of Paris gives British control over 13 American colonies
1765	Sons of Liberty form
1770	Battle of Golden Hill: Sons of Liberty vs the British
1774	New York 'Tea Party' – tax rebels empty an English tea clipper into New York harbour
1776	American Revolutionary War begins. British HQ in New York. Declaration of Independence read at Bowling Green in July
1783	Treaty of Paris ends war
1785	New York is named capital of the United States
1789	George Washington is sworn in as first US president at Federal Hall
1790	Philadelphia is named capital of the United States.

1797	Albany takes over as capital of New York State
1807	Robert Fulton launches his first steamboat, which establishes trade routes along which many New Yorkers' fortunes lie
1827	Slavery in New York is abolished
1848	Start of first great immigrant waves
1861	Civil War. New York joins the Union cause
1868	The first 'El' – elevated railway – opens
1869	'Black Friday' on Wall Street
1886	The Statue of Liberty is unveiled
1892	Ellis Island opens
1904	The IRT line opens – New York's first subway
1919	Prohibition! The 18th Amendment bans alcohol
1929	The Stock Market crashes; the Great Depression begins
1930	Chrysler Building finished – world's tallest
1931	Empire State Building finished – world's tallest
1933	Prohibition ends. Fiorello La Guardia becomes mayor
1954	Ellis Island is closed down
1964	Race riots in Harlem and Brooklyn
1973	World Trade Center finished – world's tallest
1975	New York is bankrupt. Saved by federal loan
1980	John Lennon is murdered outside the Dakota
1987	Stock market crashes
1990	David Dinkins, New York's first black mayor, takes office
1993	Terrorist bomb damages the World Trade Center
SEPT. 11. **2001**	HIJACKED " / PLANES BRING DOWN " " "

11

PEOPLE & EVENTS FROM HISTORY

John Pierpont Morgan

John Pierpont Morgan (1837–1913)

Banker J P Morgan did everything with his money from founding the Pierpont Morgan Library (► 55) to saving New York – in 1907 he and the US Treasury bought $25m of gold to rescue the city from bankruptcy. His millions derived from European investors in New York's 19th-century boomtime. He fielded those fortunes and watched over the founding of the US Steel Corporation.

TAMMANY HALL AND 'BOSS' TWEED

Tammany Hall was dedicated to fictional Iroquois chief 'St Tammany', in a spoof on the kind of upper crust fraternities William Marcy 'Boss' Tweed and his cronies despised. A famous and typical Tweed extortion was the construction of the New York County Courthouse, which cost the city $14 million dollars – $2 million for the building, and $12 million pocket lining for the Tweed Ring. Bribery was routine for them. They bought votes with jobs and cash, and tried to buy – for $500,000 – the City Hall clerk who eventually shopped them. Tweed escaped from jail and fled, but was apprehended by Spanish police who recognised him from the Thomas Nast caricatures the *New York Times* had persisted in running. Altogether, the Tweed Ring defrauded New York out of some $200 million.

NEW YORK FORTUNES

Certain names, enshrined in street names, foundations, and cultural institutions, are inescapable in New York. Who were they?

John Jacob Astor (1763–1848) was a baddie. In 1834, he started investing the fortune he'd made in the fur trade in high-rent slums, squeezing pennies out of tenement dwellers while sucking up to high society. This made him the world's richest man at his death. The best thing he did was found the Public Library.

Andrew Carnegie (1835–1919) emigrated from Scotland, began as a cotton worker, and amassed vast fortunes through iron, coal and steel, ships and rail. Self-interest was not Carnegie's motivation. The $2 million for Carnegie Hall was the least of his gifts – libraries, trusts and charities benefited from his belief that to die rich is to die in disgrace.

Henry Clay Frick (1849–1919) ►41.

Cornelius Vanderbilt (1794–1877) 'Commodore' Vanderbilt started with a ferry and ended with $105 million, which made him the richest ever American at the time. He converted the Staten Island Ferry into a steamship empire, then got diverted into railways (► 36). After his death, son Cornelius (1843–99) doubled his money.

NEW YORK
how to organise your time

ITINERARIES

The best way to do New York is by not trying to do everything. You'll be so blinkered and exhausted, you'll miss what makes this a truly great city – things like the pace, the people, the chutzpah, the sights between the sights, the sudden vista of an avenue opening up like a sun-drenched canyon. In this spirit, we offer the following as guidelines for hanging a holiday on. It doesn't matter if you miss half the stops ...

ITINERARY ONE	**LOWER MANHATTAN**
Morning	Ellis Island (►26)
	Statue of Liberty (►25)
	Brooklyn Bridge (►29)
Lunchtime	Battery Park City (► panel)
Afternoon	South Street Seaport (►27)
	Walk through Financial District to:
Sunset	The World Trade Center (►28) on West Side
	or Brooklyn Bridge on East Side
ITINERARY TWO	**MIDTOWN**
Morning	Museum of Modern Art (►38)
	Rockefeller Center (►37)
Lunchtime	Grand Central Terminal (►36)
Afternoon	United Nations (►51)
	Walk through midtown to Macy's (►71)
Sunset	Empire State Building (►33)
ITINERARY THREE	**MUSEUM MILE**
Morning	Metropolitan Museum of Art (►44)
Lunchtime	Central Park (►40)
Afternoon	Whitney Museum of American Art (►42)
	The Frick Collection (►41)
Sunset	Across the Park to the Lincoln Center (►39)

ITINERARIES

ITINERARY FOUR	**UPTOWN-DOWNTOWN**
Morning	Solomon R Guggenheim Museum (►45) Cooper-Hewitt Museum of Design (►46)
Lunchtime	Bus M1, 2, 3, 18 down Fifth Avenue to Astor Place
Afternoon	Greenwich Village (►31) Guggenheim SoHo, SoHo galleries, SoHo shopping (►45, 56 and 70)

The Empire State Building

When to do it

If you do the last tour on a Monday, Wednesday, Friday or Saturday, get off the bus at Union Square for a lunch from the Greenmarket stalls (►32). If you also want to see the work in SoHo's art galleries, and have until 10PM for the downtown Gugg (uptown's open till 8, but closed on Tuesday), Saturday is prime, though you'll also find the Village swarming. Avoid Sunday, when the Cooper-Hewitt is closed in the morning, and many SoHo galleries never open at all. Monday is no-go day for Tour Three – you'll find all the doors closed.

Battery Park City

Battery Park City is still being built on 92 acres of landfill along the Hudson, and is due to be finished around the same time as the century. Cesar Pelli's World Financial Center forms a part of it, but you may care to explore the residential areas of this futuristic city-within-a-city, especially the Esplanade (off Liberty Street) – over a mile of waterside stroll (or running track, as you'll see), with fine views of the harbour and New Jersey.

15

WALKS

INFORMATION

Distance 3 miles
Time 3 hours
Start point World Trade Center
🚇 A12
🚆 N, R, 1, 9 Cortlandt St
End point Greenwich Village
🚇 B9
🚆 1, 9 Christopher St/
Sheridan Square

Brooklyn Bridge walkway

DOWNTOWN HIGHLIGHTS

Turn your back on the twin towers of the WTC, pass Century 21 department store to your left on Cortlandt Street, and head north up Broadway. As you approach City Hall Park on the right, look left just past Barclay Street for the Gothic 'Cathedral of Commerce', the Woolworth Building. Still on Broadway, City Hall followed by the Tweed Courthouse comes into view on your right.

Walk east through the park and catch a vista of Brooklyn Bridge. Continue north up Centre Street. You now come to Cass Gilbert's gilt-pyramid-crowned US Courthouse on Foley Square at the southeast corner of Federal Plaza on your left, the neo-classical New York County Courthouse past Pearl Street on the right, then, past Hogan Street and the Criminal Courts (The Tombs).

Another block, and here's gaudy Canal Street, which you follow east to Mulberry Street (for more of a taste of Chinatown, detour around this area). Continue north up this artery of Little Italy (you'll need an espresso – Caffe Roma on the corner of Broome Street is recommended), and veer west on Prince Street. After two blocks, you're in the Cast Iron Historic District of SoHo. Look at the Little Singer Building (above Kate's Paperie) opposite as you cross Broadway, and there's the SoHo Guggenheim on the right. Take any route you please west through the cobbled streets of SoHo, heading north on any of these from Mercer to MacDougal to cross Houston Street. Three blocks later, you reach Washington Square, centre of New York University.

Fifth Avenue starts at the north side. Look at gated Washington Square Mews (first right), turn left on W8th Street (see MacDougal Alley, first left), and right onto Avenue of the Americas (Sixth Avenue). On the left is the crazily turreted Jefferson Market Library. Keep heading west and follow your nose (and page 31) to Greenwich Village, perhaps lunching at Mappamondo (✉ 11 Abingdon Square).

WALKS

MIDTOWN'S GREATEST HITS

Madison Square Garden is behind Penn Station as you exit the subway, not a garden at all, but a concrete cylinder for sports and concerts. Head two blocks uptown, then take 34th Street east one block to Herald Square, Macy's and Manhattan Mall. Toward the end of the next block, look up to your right. You're underneath the Empire State Building.

Head north up Fifth Avenue. Six blocks brings you to the Beaux-Arts magnificence of the New York Public Library, with Bryant Park behind. Go east on 42nd Street until you reach Grand Central Terminal, and on the southwest corner of Park Avenue is the Whitney's outpost in the Philip Morris Building. After a look in the Terminal (The Oyster Bar or the café provide refreshment), continue east a block and a half and on the left you'll see the Chrysler Building. Circumnavigate the Terminal, hitting Park Avenue again at 46th Street, with the MetLife (Pan Am) building at your back.

A few blocks north you'll find the precursors of the Manhattan skyline, Lever House (northwest of 53rd Street), and Ludwig Mies van der Rohe's Seagram Building (east side, 52–53rd Street). Go west on 53rd Street, south on Madison Avenue to 50th Street and veer west. Here's Saks Fifth Avenue and St Patrick's Cathedral, on the right. Straight ahead is the vast Rockefeller Center. If you have energy, the nearby Museum of Modern Art could wrap up your tour.

Live window display, Macy's

THE SIGHTS

- Madison Square Garden
- Macy's (►71)
- Empire State Building (►33)
- Fifth Avenue
- NY Public Library (►34)
- Bryant Park (►58)
- Whitney at Philip Morris (►42)
- Grand Central Terminal (►36)
- Chrysler Building (►35)
- MetLife Building (►51)
- Lever House, Seagram Building (►51)
- St Patrick's Cathedral (►52)
- Rockefeller Center (►37)
- Museum of Modern Art (►38)

INFORMATION

Distance 3 miles
Time 2 hours
Start point Madison Square Garden
✚ C7
🚇 1, 9 34th St/Penn Station
End point Rockefeller Center
✚ E5
🚇 B, D, F 47–50th St/ Rockefeller Center

17

EVENING STROLLS

INFORMATION

Museum Mile
Distance 2 miles
Time 1–2 hours
Start point 96th St at Lexington
🚇 H2
Ⓜ 6 96th St
End point Fifth Ave at Central
Park South
🚇 E5
Ⓜ N, R Fifth Ave

The East Village
Distance 2 miles
Time 1–2 hours
Start point Houston St at 2nd Ave
🚇 D10
Ⓜ F Second Ave
End point Greenwich Village
🚇 B9
Ⓜ A, C, E, B, D, F, Q W4th St

Park Avenue

MUSEUM MILE – A STROLL DOWN FIFTH AVENUE

If it's summer, you may wish to start in the early evening – around 6PM – and add a Central Park preamble, using the entrance just north of the Met at 85th Street, and perhaps watching the competitive softball on the Great Lawn. Otherwise, this stroll starts on Lexington Avenue at 96th Street, where, if it's dark, you may not wish to linger too long. Immediately you head west, however, the neighbourhood improves. This section of Park Avenue is called Carnegie Hill, and from here on, this walk takes you through Manhattan's most expensive and desirable zip codes. When you reach Central Park, turn left down Fifth Avenue and just gaze at the fantastic façades, many of them still private homes. Another half dozen blocks, and there's the magnificent Metropolitan Museum of Art, then the Frick appears, followed by the fabulous Romanesque-Byzantine style Temple Emanu-El (✉ 1 E65th St), one of the world's largest synagogues and home of New York's oldest Reform congregation. Don't miss that round window.

THE EAST VILLAGE

Coming up from the subway on to the wasteland of Houston Street by Second Avenue is not an aesthetic experience, but as you take off north, you'll quickly get the feel of this land of the hip. On the right is Lucky Chengs, on the left Little Rickie's, followed by bars, restaurants, intriguing shops, and boring stores. That block of 5th Street to the west is where exteriors for the NYPD Blue precinct are shot; the next block, 6th Street, is entirely filled with identical Indian restaurants with Christmas light décor. St Mark's Place (8th St) is the nerve centre of the neighbourhood. Go east one block to see the resurrected Tompkins Square Park, now surrounded by restaurants and bars (come back for a thorough exploration of Alphabet City – Avenues A to D were no-go areas not long ago). Go west all the way, and see how the punk funkiness gradually gives way to student pseudo-hipness, then to touristy fake coolness.

Organised Sightseeing

A choice of tours The classic way to orientate yourself and get an eyeful of the skyline is to hop on a **Circle Line Cruise** (☎212/563 3200), which circumnavigates Manhattan for three hours, with commentary. Pricier, shorter, but more dramatic, is a helicopter tour from **Island Helicopters** (☎212/683 4575), which scrapes the skyscrapers for between 7 and 35 miles. In between these extremes, slip the bus rides organised by **Gray Line** (☎212/397 2620), which include Trolley Tours on replicas of 1930s trolleys, and many standard coach-ride-with-commentary orientation trips. **New York Doubledecker** (☎212/967 6008), meanwhile, ferries you around town in a transplanted London scarlet double-decker bus.

A Circle Line cruise boat

Walking tours Many of Seth Kamil and Ed O'Donnell's **Big Onion Walking Tours** (☎212/439 1090) are back door gastronomic odysseys. But this entertaining duo also offer things like the 'Riot and Mayhem' tour of civil unrest sites. Another personalised, neighbourhood-crunching operation is **Adventure on a Shoestring** (☎212/265 2663), which has been leading small groups of walking tours for over 20 years. '**Wild Man' Steve Brill** (☎718/291 6825) leads may be the most surprising tours of all – around the Manhattan wilderness areas, with folkloric and ecological asides.

Cultural tours If you want insight into the arts, there are several backstage tours. **Backstage on Broadway** (☎212/575 8065) has actors giving talks in daytime theatres, while the **Metropolitan Opera** (☎212/769 7020) and **Radio City Music Hall** (☎212/632 4041) both allow you into the workings. Certain of the **Art Tours of Manhattan** (☎609/921 2647) and the **SoHo Art Tours** (☎212/431 8005) do a similar sort of thing with art, scheduling visits into the studios and lofts of actual artists. Also, the first crew will customise a visit to one of the major collections. **Literary Tours of Greenwich Village** (☎212/924 0239) retrace the steps of past authors, Poe to Thomas.

19

EXCURSIONS

Brooklyn Heights

INFORMATION

Start point Grand Army Plaza
✚ Off G14
🚇 2, 3 Grand Army Plaza

Brooklyn Museum
✉ 200 Eastern Parkway
☎ 718/638 5000
🕐 Wed–Sun 10–5
♿ Good
🎟 Cheap

Prospect Park
☎ 718/788 0055
(recorded info)
♿ Good

Boathouse Visitor Center
🚇 D, Q Prospect Park
☎ 718/788 8549

Brooklyn Botanic Garden
✉ 1000 Washington Ave
☎ 718/622 4433
🕐 Apr–Sep, Tue–Fri 8–6,
weekends 10–6; Oct–Mar,
Tue–Fri 8–4:30, weekends
10–4:30
🍴 Café
♿ Good
🎟 Free

A BIT OF BROOKLYN

A separate city until 1898, this 71-square-mile borough of well over 2 million souls is intimately connected to Manhattan, yet is different – as even a superficial exploration proves.

Exit the subway at Grand Army Plaza, a vast oval traffic circus dominated by the Arc de Triomphe-like Soldiers' and Sailors' Arch, which functions as gateway to Prospect Park. Designers Olmsted and Vaux felt this park, opened in 1867, was better than their earlier Central Park. Inside is near-rural woodland and meadow, and the exquisite Brooklyn Botanic Garden with its Elizabethan Knot Garden, its Japanese Garden, its Conservatory, and the Fragrance Garden with braille signs for the blind. Park Rangers give tours of the entire park, departing from the Boathouse.

On the park's northeast corner is the Brooklyn Museum, containing over 1.5 million pieces of art. Intended by McKim, Mead & White to be the biggest museum in the world, it has turned out to be the seventh largest in the US, with collections from pre-Columbian (First Floor) to 58 Rodin sculptures (Fifth Floor), and what's considered the best Egyptian collection outside the British Museum (and Egypt).

Of course, ignoring the rest of Brooklyn is like visiting only Central Park and the Met, but it's a big place ... For a flavour, stroll around leafy, middle-class Park Slope, northwest of the park.

EXCURSIONS

STATEN ISLAND

Many Staten Islanders would like to secede from the city – why should they share New York's problems and taxes, they argue, when they not only have their own discrete, rather rural community, but are also completely ignored by all four other boroughs? Whatever their political status however, their island is pure pleasure to visit, especially in summer when all manner of events are laid on. Once you've enjoyed the famous ferry ride, buses are the best way to get around.

Snug Harbor is a work-in-progress – a visual and performance arts centre in an 80-acre park of 28 historic buildings. Long established here are the Children's Museum and the Botanical Garden, as well as a couple of performance venues and a restored row of Greek Revival houses. Both this and historic Richmondtown have a programme of summer fairs, concerts, and other events. In the dead centre of the island, Richmondtown traces 200 years of New York history through restored buildings, crafts workshops, and costumed re-enactments. There's no better place to get a picture of how New York evolved.

A good use for a spare subway token is to take a ride on the Staten Island train, which takes about 40 minutes to go its picturesque route from the ferry to Tottenville and includes a great view of the mighty Brooklyn-bound Verrazano-Narrows Bridge.

INFORMATION

✚ Off A14
⛴ Staten Island Ferry (➤ 53)

Richmondtown
✉ 441 Clarke Ave
☎ 718/351 1611
🕐 Apr–Dec, Wed–Sun 1–5; Jan–Mar, Wed–Fri 1–5
🚌 S74
🍴 Tavern
♿ Moderate
💲 Cheap

Snug Harbor Cultural Center
✉ 1000 Richmond Terrace
☎ 718/448 2500
🕐 8AM–dusk
🚌 S40
🍴 Melville's Café
♿ Good
💲 Free

Snug Harbor

WHAT'S ON

(Also ▶58, 60, 79 and 82)

JANUARY/FEBRUARY	Chinese New Year parades: ✉ Chinatown
MARCH	St Patrick's Day Parade (17 March): ✉ Fifth Ave, 44–86th streets
MARCH/APRIL	Easter Parade: ✉ Fifth Ave, 44–59th streets
APRIL	Baseball season starts (till Oct): ✉ Yankee and Shea stadiums
MAY	Ninth Avenue International Food Festival: ✉ Ninth Ave, 37–57th streets
	Martin Luther King Day Parade (3rd Sun): ✉ Fifth Ave, 44–86th streets
JUNE	Metropolitan Opera parks concerts: ☎ 212/362 6000
	JVC Jazz Festival, various venues: ☎ 212/787 2020
	Lesbian and Gay Pride Parade: ☎ 212/463 9030
4 JULY	Independence Day (▶82)
JULY–AUGUST	Shakespeare in the Park, Delacorte Theater: ☎ 212/598 7100
	NY Philharmonic parks concerts: ☎ 212/360 1333
AUGUST	Harlem Week: ☎ 212/427 7200
AUGUST–SEPTEMBER	Lincoln Center Out-of-Doors Festival (▶82): ☎ 212/875 5400
	US Open Tennis Championships: ☎ 718/760 6200
SEPTEMBER	Feast of San Gennaro, Little Italy: ☎ 212/226 9546
SEPTEMBER–OCTOBER	New York Film Festival, Lincoln Center: ☎ 212/875 5050
OCTOBER	Blessing of the Animals, St John the Divine: ☎ 212/316 7400
	Columbus Day Parade: ✉ Fifth Ave, 44–86th streets
	Halloween Parade, Greenwich Village: ☎ 914/758 5519
NOVEMBER	NYC Marathon, Verrazano-Narrows Bridge: ☎ 212/860 4455
	Macy's Thanksgiving Day Parade: ☎ 212/494 5432
DECEMBER	Tree Lighting Ceremony, Rockefeller Centre: ☎ 212/632 3975
NEW YEAR'S EVE	Times Square, ball drops at midnight: ☎ 212/768 1560

NEW YORK's
top 25 sights

*The sights are numbered from
south to north through the city.*

1

CONEY ISLAND

HIGHLIGHTS

- Aquarium
- The Boardwalk
- The Cyclone
- Nathan's Famous hot dogs
- The Sideshow
- Mermaid Parade, June
- Fleamarket

INFORMATION

- ✚ Off A14
- ✉ Surf Ave, Boardwalk, Brooklyn; Aquarium W8th St, Surf Ave
- ☎ Aquarium 718/265 3474
- 🕐 Aquarium 10–5 daily, summer weekends and holidays till 7PM
- 🍴 Cafeteria at Aquarium
- Ⓢ B, D, F Stillwell Ave/Coney Island, W8th St, NY Aquarium
- 🚌 B36, B68
- ♿ Good; aquarium very good
- 💲 Free; aquarium moderate

❝*Half slummy neighbourhood with the skeleton of a fairground, half sunny seaside resort with a peach of a boardwalk, Coney Island is redolent with other people's memories.*❞

Nathan's and the Cyclone At the end of the last century, Coney Island on a peak day played host to a million people, attracted by Brooklyn's seaside air and by Luna Park, Dreamland and Steeplechase Park fairgrounds. By 1921, a boardwalk and the subway had joined the list of attractions, then the World's Fair of 1939–40 added the biggest draw of all, the 'Parachute jump'. At the end of this century, that machine is still there, a rusted ghost like a giant spider on stilts, and the glory days of Luna Park are long since gone, yet seedy Coney Island still draws a crowd. The big dipper ride, the Cyclone, is still there, more terrifying for the possibility of collapse than for the thrill of the ride (though it's not at all bad), and Nathan's Famous hot dogs are still sold from the original site, plus cotton candy, saltwater taffy, and corn dogs (franks deep fried in cornmeal).

Fish and freakshows The New York Aquarium, watery branch of the Bronx Zoo, moved here in 1957. Roughly 10,000 creatures call it home, including beluga whales, coral, a penguin colony and five varieties of shark. It's quite as wonderful as it sounds. The boardwalk Sideshow, though boasting an elastic lady and the blockhead (he hammers nails into his brain), is not such a freak show as it sounds. It's a theatrical performance by East Village arty types.

THE STATUE OF LIBERTY

❝*Not only does the green lady symbolise the American dream of freedom, but she quite takes your breath away, however many times you've seen her photograph – and despite her surprisingly modest stature.*❞

How she grew In the late 1860s, sculptor Frédéric-Auguste Bartholdi dreamed of placing a monument to freedom in a prominent place. His dream merged with the French historian Edouard-René de Laboulaye's idea of presenting the American people with a statue celebrating freedom and the two nations' friendship. Part of the idea was to shame the repressive French government, but, apparently, New Yorkers took their freedom for granted, and it was only after Joseph Pullitzer promised to print the name of every donor in his newspaper, the *New York World*, that the city's ordinary citizens coughed up the funds to build the statue's pedestal. She was finally unveiled by President Grover Cleveland on 28 October 1886 in a ceremony from which women were banned.

Mother of exiles Emma Lazarus's stirring poem, *The New Colossus*, is engraved on the pedestal, while the tablet reads: July IV MDCCLXXVI – the date of the Declaration of Independence. Beneath her size 107 feet, she tramples the broken shackles of tyranny, and her seven-pointed crown beams liberty to the seven continents and the seven seas.

What is she made of? Gustave Eiffel practised for his later work by designing the 1,700-bar iron and steel structure which supports her. She weighs 225 tons, is 151 feet tall, has an 8-foot index finger and a skin of 300 copper plates. The torch tip towers 305 feet above sea level.

HIGHLIGHTS

- The climb to the crown
- The view from the pedestal
- Statue of Liberty Museum
- Fort Wood, the star-shaped pedestal base
- Her new centenary flame

INFORMATION

- ✚ Off A14
- ✉ Liberty Island
- ☎ 212/363 3200; ferry 212/269 5755; ticket office 212/344 7220
- 🕐 Jul–Aug daily 9–6; Sep–Jun daily 9:30–5. Closed 25 Dec
- 🍴 Cafeteria
- 🚇 1, 9 South Ferry; 4, 5 Bowling Green; N, R Whitehall St
- 🚌 M1, M6, M15 South Ferry
- ♿ Few
- 🎫 Cheap
- ↔ Ellis Island (➤ 26) (joint admission), Staten Island Ferry (➤ 53), Battery Park City (➤ 15)
- ❓ Audio tours available
- ⛴ Ferry departs Battery Park South Ferry (A13). Tickets from Castle Clinton National Monument, Battery Park

3

ELLIS ISLAND

INFORMATION

- ✚ Off A14
- ✉ Ellis Island
- ☎ 212/363 3200
- ◑ Jul–Aug daily 9–6;
  Sep–Jun 9:30–5.
  Closed 25 Dec
- 🍴 Café
- 🚇 1, 9 South Ferry;
  4, 5 Bowling Green;
  N, R Whitehall St
- 🚌 M1, M6, M15
- ♿ Good
- 💲 Cheap
- ↔ Statue of Liberty (➤ 25)
  (joint admission), Staten
  Island Ferry (➤ 53),
  Battery Park City (➤ 15)
- ❓ Audio tours available
- 🛳 Ferry departs Battery Park
  South Ferry (A13). Tickets
  from Castle Clinton National
  Monument, Battery Park

> **❝**One of the city's newer museums offers the near-compulsory humbling taste of how the huddled masses were not allowed to go free until they'd been herded through these halls, weighed, measured and rubber stamped.**❞**

Half of all America It was the poor who docked at Ellis Island after sometimes gruelling voyages in steerage, since first-class passage included permission to decant straight into Manhattan. Annie Moore, aged 15 and the first future American, arrived here in 1892, followed by 16 million founding fathers over the next 40 years, including such American-sounding Americans as Irving Berlin and Frank Capra. Half the population of the United States can trace their roots to an Ellis Island immigrant.

Island of tears The exhibition in the main building conveys the indignities, frustrations and, above all, fears of the arrivals. (As soon as you arrive, collect your free ticket for the half-hour film, *Island of Hope/Island of Tears*, which you'll otherwise end up missing.) You are guided around more or less the same route the millions took: from the Baggage Room, where they had to abandon all they owned; on to the enormous Registry Room, now bare not only of people, but of furniture too; and on through the series of inspection chambers where medical, mental, and political status were ascertained. The Oral History Studio brings it all to life, as former immigrants recount their experience; especially moving coupled with the poignant possessions in the 'Treasures from Home' exhibit. All this makes for a demanding few hours' sightseeing, which you'll probably be combining with the Statue of Liberty, since the ferries stop at both islands. Wear sensible shoes; bring lunch.

SOUTH STREET SEAPORT

"This reconstructed historic maritime district, with its chintzy cobbled streets, is something of a tourist trap. However, when you stroll the boardwalk on a summer's night, with the moon over the East River, you are quite glad to be a tourist."

Pier, cruise, shop, eat The seaside/cruise-ship atmosphere is what's fun at the Pier 17 Pavilion,

The Seaport in the evening

which juts 400 feet into the East River, overlooking Brooklyn Heights. It's a mall, with chain stores, bad restaurants and a Food Court, but also three storeys of charming wooden decks. The adjoining piers, 16 and 15, harbour a number of historic vessels with picturesque arrangements of rigging, plus the replica side-wheeler, *Andrew Fletcher*, and the 1885 schooner, *Pioneer*, which give harbour cruises. On land, your cash is courted by many shops, housed in the 1812 Federal-style warehouses of Schermerhorn Row – Manhattan's oldest block – and around Water, Front and Fulton streets, and also by the few remaining cafés in the old Fulton Market.

Many museums The Seaport Museum Visitors' Center acts as clearing house for all the small-scale exhibitions here. One ticket admits you to: the second-biggest sailing ship ever built, the *Peking*, the floating lighthouse, *Ambrose*, the Children's Center, the Seaport Museum Gallery, a re-creation of a 19th-century printer's shop, various walking tours, and more.

HIGHLIGHTS

- The view of Brooklyn Heights
- Richard Haas' Brooklyn Bridge mural
- Late night forays in the Fulton Fish Market (midnight–8AM)
- Boarding *Andrew Fletcher*
- Watching the Wall Street young decant into the bars around 5PM
- The *Titanic* Memorial
- The Chandlery
- Fulton Market (especially the bakeries)
- The incongruous giant bubble (tennis courts!)
- The sea breeze

INFORMATION

- ✚ B12/13
- ✉ Visitor Center, 12 Fulton St; tickets also from Pier 16
- ☎ 212/669 9424
- 🕐 Jun–Sep, daily 10–6; Oct–May, daily 10–5. Closed Thu, and 25 Dec and 1 Jan
- 🍴 Too numerous to list
- 🚇 2, 3, 4, 5, J, M, Z Fulton St; A, C Broadway/Nassau St
- 🚌 M15 Pearl/Fulton St
- ♿ Few/none
- 💲 Free–moderate
- ↔ World Trade Center (➤ 28), Brooklyn Bridge (➤ 29)
- ❓ Walking tours: 'Ship Restoration', 'Back Streets', etc

WORLD TRADE CENTER

HIGHLIGHTS

- The View
- The View on 4 July
- The rooftop promenade
- The View at sunset
- Free concerts in the Plaza
- Breakfast at Windows on the World
- The elevator ride
- The Vista hotel's health club

INFORMATION

- 🔢 A12
- ✉ World Trade Center, between Liberty and Vesey streets
- ☎ 212/435 7397
- 🕐 Jun–Sep, daily 9:30AM–11:30PM; Oct–May, daily 9:30–9:30
- 🍴 Call 212/938 1111 for Windows on the World reopening info
- Ⓜ C, E World Trade Center; 1, 9, N, R Cortlandt St
- 🚌 M10
- 🚆 PATH WTC
- ♿ Good
- 💲 Cheap–moderate
- ↔ World Financial Center (► 51), Battery Park City (► 15)

❝Not much liked when they went up (and up and up) in the 1970s, the 'twin towers' practically define the lower Manhattan skyline. Four boring buildings, the Vista hotel, and a mall complete the Center, but the view is the point.**❞**

Scary skyscrapers The twin towers are like jellyfish in that their outer covering is all that holds them together. Minoru Yamasaki's design replaced the steel skeleton of the average skyscraper with load-bearing exterior walls of vertical columns and gigantic horizontal spandrel beams. Large windows for the workers' warren inside were sacrificed. The workers themselves were nearly sacrificed in February 1993, when a terrorist bomb rocked Floor 1 WTC.

Vital statistics The towers' 110 floors rise 1,350 feet, or a quarter of a mile, supplying 10 million square feet of office space for 50,000 workers. Each tower contains 99 elevators, but the 80,000 daily visitors are allocated a single express that reaches the 107th floor of Tower Two in 58 seconds flat. Although over 1,000 people were injured in the 1993 bomb blast, the walls ran red not with blood, but with wine – over $2 million worth of bottles were blasted from the Cellar in the Sky (due to reopen in 1996).

No vertigo After they were finished in 1973, the towers attracted aerial mayhem. Philippe Petit walked a towertop-to-towertop tightrope in August 1974, for which he was arrested and ordered to do kids' shows in Central Park. A year later, Owen Quinn parachuted off. Recklessness charges were dropped. Finally, in May 1977, George Willig, using crampons of his own design, climbed up a tower. The city sued for a quarter million, but accepted $1.10.

BROOKLYN BRIDGE

❝The view from the Bridge is spectacular, but the structure itself, with its twin Gothic towers and ballet of cables, means the first Manhattan–Brooklyn link fulfils beautifully its symbolic role of affording entry into new worlds of opportunity.❞

Killer bridge In 1869, before construction had even started, the original engineer, John Roebling, had his foot crushed by a ferry and died of gangrene three weeks later. His son, Washington, took over the project, only to succumb to the bends and subsequent paralysis. Washington's wife, Emily Warren, finished overseeing the construction, during which 20 workmen died in various nasty accidents. Then, on 30 May 1883, a few days after the opening, a woman fell over, screamed, and set off a 20,000-person stampede, which claimed 12 more lives. Robert Odlum's was the first non-accidental Bridge-related death. He jumped off for a bet in 1885 and died from internal bleeding later.

Bridge of sighs Now, the occasional leaper chooses the cable walk as their last, but things are mostly peaceful. The best time and direction to walk the renovated (in 1983) footpath is east from Brooklyn to Manhattan at dusk. The sun sets behind Liberty Island and, as you stroll on, downtown looms larger and larger, the sky darkens to cobalt, the lights go on, the skyline goes sparkly, and you are swallowed into the metropolis. It's a transcendental half hour. Although you'll almost certainly be fine, it's still not a good plan to walk the bridge toward and into Brooklyn at night, especially carrying cameras or other tourist paraphernalia.

HIGHLIGHTS

- The walk to Manhattan
- The panorama of NY buildings
- The cables – each of 5,282 wires
- Jehovah's Witnesses' Watchtower HQ
- Cars hurtling, 6 yards below your feet
- Cyclists hurtling, 6 inches from your face

INFORMATION

- ✚ C13
- ✉ Walkway entrance is across Park Row from City Hall Park
- Ⓠ 4, 5, 6 Brooklyn Bridge/City Hall; J, M, Z Chambers St
- 🚌 M1, M6
- ♿ Very good
- 🎫 Free
- ↔ South Street Seaport (➤ 27)

The Lower Manhattan skyline from beneath Brooklyn Bridge

29

CHINATOWN

INFORMATION

- C11/12
- The area roughly delineated by Worth St/East Broadway, the Bowery, Grand St, and Centre St
- Opening hours are long, though many restaurants shut around 10PM
- About 350 of them
- J, M, Z, N, R, 6, A, C, E, 1, 9 Canal St; B, D Grand St
- M1, B51
- None
- Little Italy (► 54), Lower East Side Tenement Museum (► 55), SoHo Guggenheim (► 45)
- General tours: Chinatown History Museum, ☎ 212/619 4785; Chinese herbal medicine tours: Open Center, ☎ 212/219 2527

❝ *New York's Chinatown, the largest in the West, encroaches on what remains of Little Italy and the Jewish Lower East Side, even on Hispanic 'Loisaida'. Wander here, and you're humbled by the sight of a lifestyle which, making no concessions to the visitor, remains forever opaque.* **❞**

Going west Prefiguring the movement of emigrants from the devolved Russia and Eastern Europe of today, Chinese people first came to New York in the late 19th century, looking to work a while, make some money, and return home. But, by 1880 or so, some 10,000 men – mostly Cantonese railroad workers decamped from California – had got stranded between Canal, Worth and Baxter Streets. Tongs – sort of secret mafia operations, similar to the Triads – were formed, and still keep order today, over some 150,000 Chinese, Taiwanese, Vietnamese, Burmese and Singaporeans. New York, incidentally, has two more Chinatowns, in Flushing, Queens, and Eighth Avenue, Brooklyn, with a further 150,000-odd inhabitants.

A closed world Although you may happily wander its colourful, slightly manic, streets, you will never penetrate Chinatown. Many of its denizens never learn English, never leave its environs, never have left its environs, and never wish to. The 600 factories and 350 restaurants keep them in work, then there are the tea shops, mah-jong parlours, herbalists, fishmongers, and the highest bank-to-citizen ratio in New York, in which Chinese stash their wages (normally not more than $10–$20,000 a year) to save for the 'eight bigs' (car, TV, video recorder, fridge, camera, phone, washing machine and furniture), to send home, or eventually to invest in a business of their own.

GREENWICH VILLAGE

This tooth-achingly picturesque, human-scale neighbourhood of brownstones and actual trees is the other romantic image of Manhattan (second to the skyline), familiar from sitcoms and movies. Its dense streets are rewarding to wander.

What village? Named after Greenwich, southeast London, by the British colonists who settled here at the end of the 17th century. The 18th and early 19th centuries were when the wealthy founders of New York society took refuge here from smallpox, cholera and yellow fever.

Bohemia, academe, jazz When the élite moved on and up, the bohemian invasion began, pioneered by Edgar Allan Poe, who moved to 85 W3rd Street in 1845. Fellow literary habitués included: Mark Twain, O Henry, Walt Whitman, F Scott Fitzgerald, Eugene O'Neill, John Dos Passos, and ee cummings. New York University arrived in Washington Square in 1831 and grew into the country's largest private university. Post World War II, bohemia became beatnik; a group of abstract artists centred around Jackson Pollock, Mark Rothko and Willem de Kooning, also found a home here.

Freedom parades Café Society, where Billie Holiday made her 1938 debut, was one of the first non-racially-segregated clubs in New York. Thirty years later, a different kind of discrimination was challenged, when police raided the Stonewall Inn on 28 June 1969, arresting gay men for illegally buying drinks and setting off the Stonewall Riots – the birth of the Gay Rights Movement. The Inn stood on Christopher Street, which became the main drag (no pun intended) of New York's gay community and ranked with San Francisco for excitement.

HIGHLIGHTS

- Cafés
- Jazz clubs
- Washington Square Park
- NYC's narrowest house (75 Bedford St)
- The West (of Hudson St) Village
- The Halloween Parade (31 Oct)
- Jefferson Market Library
- Balducci's (the grocers)
- Minetta Lane
- Carmine St pool (Clarkson/Seventh Ave S)

Washington Memorial Arch

INFORMATION

- ✚ B9–C9
- ✉ East to west from Broadway to Hudson St; north to south from 14th St to Houston St
- 🍴 Thousands
- 🚇 A, C, E, B, D, F W4th St; 1, 9 Christopher St
- 🚌 M10
- 🚉 PATH Christopher St
- ♿ None
- ↔ SoHo (▶ 54)

31

11

NEW YORK PUBLIC LIBRARY

INFORMATION

- ✚ D6
- ✉ 476 Fifth Ave, 42nd St
- ☎ 212/869 8089
- ◉ Thu–Sat 10–6; Tue–Wed 11–7:30. Closed holidays
- 🍴 Snack kiosks outside (not winter)
- 🚇 4, 5, 6, 7, S 42 St Grand Central
- 🚌 M101, M102
- 🚆 Metro North, Grand Central
- ♿ Good (also see below)
- 🆓 Free
- ↔ Grand Central Terminal (➤ 36), Chrysler Building (➤ 35), Empire State Building (➤ 33), Bryant Park (➤ 58)
- ❓ Tours: 11AM and 2PM daily Notable branches include: the Andrew Heiskell Library for the Blind and Physically Handicapped (✉ 40 W20th St) and the Library for the Performing Arts (✉ 40 Lincoln Plaza)

> **"**Why are we sending you to a library on your holidays? Because the NY Public Library's Central Research Building is a great, white, hushed palace, quite beautiful to behold even if you have no time to open a book. **"**

The building Carrère and Hastings (see the Frick) were the architects responsible for what is generally thought the city's best representative of the Beaux-Arts style – the sumptuous yet classical French school that flourished in New York's 'gilded age': about 1880–1920. A pair of lions, which Mayor La Guardia christened Patience and Fortitude, flank the majestic stair that leads directly into the barrel-vaulted, carved white marble temple of Astor Hall. The lions are themselves flanked by fountains, 'Truth' and 'Beauty', which echo the site's previous (1845–99) incarnation, as the Croton Reservoir, supplying the city's water. Behind this briefly stood New York's version of London's Crystal Palace, built for the first American World's Fair in 1853. Like the London one, it burned down. Inside, see temporary exhibitions in the Gottesman Hall, and look up! The carved oak ceiling is sublime; read in the two-block-long Main Reading Room; see library collection rarities in the Salomon Room, and don't miss the Richard Haas murals of NYC publishing houses in the De Witt Wallace Periodical Room.

The books The Library owns over 15 million books, most living in the 82 branches. This building is dedicated to research. The CATNYP computer, complete with dumb waiter, can disgorge any of the 16 million manuscripts or 3 million books from the 92 miles of stacks in ten minutes flat.

Top: the reading room

CHRYSLER BUILDING

❝*Which is your favourite New York building?' goes the annoying yet perennial question. As it turns out, nine out of ten people who express a preference choose the Chrysler Building over other brands. This should surprise nobody who gazes on it.*❞

King for a year The tower, commissioned from William Van Alen by Walter Chrysler (who asked for something 'taller than the Eiffel Tower'), won the world's tallest building competition in 1930 ... until the Empire State Building went up the following year. Van Alen had been almost pipped to the post by Craig Severance's Bank of Manhattan tower at 40 Wall Street, when his rival, aware of the unofficial race, slung on an extra two feet. Unbeknownst to Severance, though, Van Alen was secretly constructing a 123-foot stainless steel spire, which he 'posted' out through the 925-foot roof, beating the 927-footer hands down. It's sort of ironic that the best view of the art deco beauty's top is now gained from the observatory at the Empire State.

Multi-storey car Every detail of the 77-storey building evokes the motor car – a 1929 Chrysler Plymouth, to be exact. The winged steel gargoyles are modelled on its radiator caps; other of the building's stepped setbacks carry stylised hubcaps, and the entire spire resembles a radiator grille; and this ain't no Toyota. The golden age of motoring is further evoked by the stunning lobby, which you can visit – ostensibly to view the Con Edison (New York's utilities company) conservation exhibit, but really to see the red marble, granite and chrome interior, surmounted by the 97 by 100-foot mural depicting industrial scenes and celebrating 'transportation'.

HIGHLIGHTS

- The spire
- The ceiling mural
- The elevator cabs
- The fourth setback gargoyles
- The African marble lobby

INFORMATION

- ✚ E6
- ✉ 405 Lexington Ave/42nd St
- 🕐 Mon–Fri 7AM–6PM. Closed holidays
- 🚇 4, 5, 6, 7, S 42nd St, Grand Central
- 🚌 M101, M102
- 🚆 Metro North, Grand Central
- ♿ Good
- 🎫 Free
- ↔ Empire State Building (➤ 33)

The pinnacle of success

GRAND CENTRAL TERMINAL

HIGHLIGHTS

- The Main Concourse ceiling
- The Oyster Bar
- The bar over the Main Concourse
- Mercury on the 42nd St façade
- The Clock
- The free art installations
- The 75-foot arched windows
- The Grand Staircase
- The uneven Tennessee marble floor
- Municipal Arts Society tours

INFORMATION

- E6
- Park Ave, 42nd St
- 212/532 4900
- 5:30AM–1:30AM daily
- Restaurant, café/bar, snack bars
- 4, 5, 6, 7, S 42nd St, Grand Central
- M101, 102 Grand Central
- Metro North, Grand Central
- Good
- Free
- NY Public Library (➤ 34), Chrysler Building (➤ 35), Empire State Building (➤ 33), Bryant Park (➤ 58)
- Tours: Wed 12.30PM. Meet by Chemical Bank in Main Concourse

❝Don't call it a station. All tracks terminate here, which makes this railway mecca a far grander entity. The Beaux-Arts building bustles like no place else; stand here long enough, and the entire world passes by.❞

Heart of the nation 'Grand Central Station!' bellowed (erroneously) the 1937 opening of the eponymous NBC radio drama; 'Beneath the glitter and swank of Park Avenue ... Crossroads of a million private lives!... Heart of the nation's greatest city...'. And so it is, and has been since 1871, when the first, undersized version was opened by Commodore Cornelius Vanderbilt, who had bought up all the city's railroads, just like on a giant Monopoly board. See him in bronze below Jules-Alexis Coutans' allegorical statuary on the main (south, 42nd Street) façade. The current building dates from 1913 and is another Beaux-Arts glory, its design modelled partly on the Paris Opéra by architects Warren and Wetmore. William Wilgus was the logician responsible for traffic-marshalling, while Reed & Stem were the overall engineers. Recent cleaning of the Main Concourse ceiling has re-revealed the stunning sight of 2,500 'stars' in a cerulean sky, with medieval-style zodiac signs by French artist Paul Helleu.

Meeting under the clock The fame of the four-faced clock atop the information booth is out of all proportion to its size. (You may remember the scene in the movie *The Fisher King* where thousands of commuters fell into synchronised waltzing around it.) Beneath the clock, and the ground, is a warren of 32 miles of tracks, tunnels, and vaulted chambers, in one of which the famed Oyster Bar resides. Be careful what you say here – the acoustics are a whispering gallery.

ROCKEFELLER CENTER

❝*This small village of famous art deco buildings provides many of those 'gee this is New York' moments: in winter when you see ice-skaters ringed by the flags of the UN, or anytime over cocktails in the Rainbow Room.*❞

Prometheus is here The buildings' bible, Willensky and White's *AIA Guide to NYC*, calls the 19-building Rockefeller Center: 'The greatest urban complex of the 20th century.' It is 'the heart of New York,' agreed the Landmarks Commission in 1985. So the architectural importance of the Center – and especially the elongated ziggurat GE Building (better known as the RCA Building) – is beyond dispute, but it's still easy to enjoy the place. Rest on a Channel Gardens bench, enjoy the seasonal foliage, and gaze on the lower plaza, the rink, and Paul Manship's *Prometheus*. The Channel is a reference to the English Channel, since these sloping gardens separate La Maison Française from the British Empire Building.

Rockefeller the Younger The realisation of John D Rockefeller Junior's grand scheme to outdo dad (Mister Standard Oil) provided work for a quarter of a million souls during the Depression. In 1957, Marilyn Monroe detonated the dynamite for the Time & Life buildings' foundations, and the Center was still growing into the 1970s.

Conan and Rockettes For many years, the NBC Studios in the GE Building hosted the hip TV talk show *Late Night* with David Letterman. Dave decamped to CBS (where he lost all cool), and Conan O'Brian was plucked from obscurity to host the spot. Over on Avenue of the Americas is Radio City Music Hall, landmark home to the Rockettes, born in 1934 and still kicking.

Atlas, *Lee Lawrie*

HIGHLIGHTS

- The GE Building, outside
- The GE Building's lobbies
- The Rainbow Room
- NBC Studio tour
- Skating in winter
- The Sea Grill restaurant
- Radio City Music Hall
- Channel Gardens
- Prometheus
- Atlas (Fifth Ave, 50–51st St)

INFORMATION

- ✚ E5
- ✉ Fifth–7th Ave, 47–52nd St
- 🕐 Various hours
- 🍴 Numerous restaurants/cafés
- Ⓜ B, D, F 47–50th streets, Rockefeller Center
- 🚌 M1, M2, M3, M4, M5, M18
- ♿ Varies
- 🎫 Free
- ↔ Mus. of Modern Art (➤ 38)
- ❓ Radio City tours, ☎ 212/632 4041; NBC Studio tours, ☎ 212/644 3056

37

15

MUSEUM OF MODERN ART

INFORMATION

- E5
- 11 W53rd St
- 212/708 7500
- Fri–Tue 11–6, Thur 11–9. Closed 25 Dec
- Restaurant
- B, D, E Seventh Ave; E, F Fifth Ave
- M5, M6, M7, M18
- Few
- Moderate

MoMA's modern façade

"A great collection housed in a cool building – literally in summer. The film programme is practically the final fling of repertory cinema in New York; even the shop and the popular restaurant are modern and arty."

Van Gogh to Man Ray Founded on the 1931 bequest of Lillie P Bliss, which consisted of 235 works, the MoMA collections now amount to about 100,000 pieces of art. True to the museum's title, these include modern arts: photography, graphic design, household objects, conceptual art, and industrial design, though work from the first half of the century is better represented than the really new – go to the Whitney for that. There are four floors, plus the Abby Aldrich Rockefeller Sculpture Garden – where you can retreat from the city in the company of Rodin, Picasso and Moore. The works are arranged more or less chronologically, with temporary shows sharing the upper floors with architecture and design.

Post-Impressionists to Graffitists The collection starts late last century, with the Post-Impressionists and Fauvists: Cézanne, Van Gogh (pronounced 'van go' round here), Seurat, Gauguin, Matisse. Most movements of this century follow – Cubism, Expressionism, Futurism, Surrealism, Abstract Expressionism – up to and including Pop (Oldenburg, Dine, Rauschenberg, Warhol, of course), and the 'Graffiti' work of Keith Haring and Jean-Michel Basquiat. What was probably MoMA's most famous and important painting of all no longer hangs here. It was Picasso's 1937 *Guernica*, which, post-Franco, was given back to the Spanish.

LINCOLN CENTER

" *Strolling to the fantastically fairy-lit ten-storey Metropolitan Opera House colonnade across the Central Plaza on a winter's night is one of the most glamorous things you can do on this earth, and you don't need tickets.* **"**

West Side Story The ambitious Rockefeller-funded über-arts centre was envisaged in the late 1950s and finished in 1969, after 7,000 families and 800 businesses had been turfed out of their homes by developer Robert Moses and the John D Rockefeller millions. Much of *West Side Story* was actually shot on these streets after the demolition had begun, capturing the pain of change forever.

All the arts The 15 acres include megahouses for the biggest-scale arts, all designed by different architects in the same white travertine. The Metropolitan Opera House is the glamour queen, with her vast Marc Chagall murals, miles of red carpet, swooshes of stair, and starry chandeliers that swiftly, silently and thrillingly rise to the sky-high gold-leafed ceiling before performances. Avery Fisher Hall caught America's oldest orchestra, the NY Philharmonic, on its trajectory out of Carnegie Hall, while the Juilliard School of Music keeps it supplied with fresh maestri. The New York State Theater, housing the New York City Opera and the New York City Ballet, faces Avery Fisher across the Plaza. Two smaller theatres, the Vivian Beaumont and Mitzi Newhouse, and a more intimate concert hall, Alice Tully, plus the Walter Reade movie theatre, the little Bruno Walter Auditorium, and the Guggenheim Bandshell for outdoor summer concerts complete the pack. Over 13,500 arts fans can be swallowed simultaneously. Just don't expect to find a cab after.

HIGHLIGHTS

- Chandeliers in the Met auditorium
- Reflecting Pool with Henry Moore's *Reclining Figure*
- Lincoln Center Out-of-Doors Festival
- NY City Ballet's *Nutcracker*
- Chagall murals, Met foyer
- Thursday morning rehearsals, Avery Fisher
- New York Film Festival
- Philip Johnson's Plaza fountain
- Chamber Music Society, Alice Tully
- Annual *Messiah* singalong

INFORMATION

- ✚ D3/4
- ✉ Broadway 62nd–67th streets
- ☎ 212/875 5400, Met 212/362 6000, Avery Fisher 212/875 5030
- 🕐 Depends on performance times
- 🍴 Various restaurants, cafés, bars
- Ⓢ 1, 9 66th St Lincoln Center
- 🚌 M5, M7, M104, crosstown M66
- ♿ Good–excellent, ☎ 212/875 5350 for info
- 🔁 Depends on ticket cost; admission to Center free
- ↔ Central Park (► 40)
- ❓ Tours leave from concourse under Met daily 10–5, ☎ 212/875 5350

CENTRAL PARK

HIGHLIGHTS

- Delacorte Theater Shakespeare in the Park
- Summerstage concerts
- The bleachers at Heckscher
- Bethesda Fountain
- Wollman Rink in winter
- Strawberry Fields
- Horse-drawn carriage ride
- Swedish Cottage Marionette Theater
- Tavern on the Green

INFORMATION

❝*The park's the escape valve on the pressure cooker. Without it New York would explode – especially in summer, when the humidity tops 90 per cent, and bikers, runners, bladers, dog strollers, softball and frisbee players convene. It's a way of life.*❞

Olmsted, Vaux and the Greensward Plan In the middle of the last century, when there was no Manhattan north of 42nd Street, *New York Evening Post* editor, William Cullen Bryant, campaigned until the city invested the fortune of $5m in an 840-acre wasteland swarming with pig-farming squatters who ran bone-boiling operations. Responsible for clearing the land was journalist Frederick Law Olmsted, who, with English architect Calvert Vaux, also won the competition to design the park, with his 'Greensward Plan'. By day, Olmsted supervised the shifting of five million cubic tons of dirt; by night, he and Vaux trod the wasteland acres and designed. Night strolls above 59th Street today are not recommended.

Swings and roundabouts Start at the Dairy Information Center, and pick up a map and events list. These show the lie of the land and tell you about the Wildlife Conservation Center (the ex-Zoo), the Carousel, the playgrounds, rinks, fountains, statues, and Strawberry Fields, where John Lennon is commemorated close to the Dakota Building where he lived and was shot. But the busy life of a park rat is not recorded on maps: showing off rollerblade moves on the Mall by the Sheep Meadow; hanging out at the Heckscher Playground and Great Lawn softball leagues; doing the loop road fast, by bike; sunbathing poolside at the vast Lasker Pool in Harlem; playing rowboat dodgems on The Lake; bouldering on the outcrops of Manhattan schist...

THE FRICK COLLECTION

" *Like the Wallace Collection in London and the Musée Picasso in Paris, Henry Clay Frick's mansion is half the reason for seeing his collection. Henry bequeathed these riches to the nation as a memorial to himself – that's the kind of guy he was.* **"**

The mansion, and the man Henry Clay Frick was chairman of the Carnegie Steel Corp (US Steel). He was one of the most ruthless strike-breakers of all time and quite the nastiest industrialist of his day. Instead of any come-uppance (though there were several assassina-tion attempts), he got to commission Carrère and Hastings (who designed the NY Public Library) to build him one of the last great Beaux-Arts mansions on Fifth Avenue and fill it with an exquisite collection of 14th–19th-cen-tury Old Masters, porcelain, furniture and bronzes. Not much of the furniture is velvet-roped, so you can rest your limbs in a Louis Seize chair before a stroll in the central glass-roofed courtyard and the gorgeous garden.

What Frick bought Certain rooms of the 40-room mansion are arranged around a particular work or artist, notably the Boucher Room, just east of the entrance, and especially the Fragonard room, with the 11-painting *Progress of Love* series. There are British masters (Constable, Whistler, Turner, Gainsborough), Dutch (Vermeer, Rembrandt, Van Eyck, Hals), Italian (Titian, Bellini, Veronese) and Spanish (El Greco, Velázquez, Goya). Interspersed are Limoges enamel and Chinese porcelain, Persian carpets and Marie Antoinette's furniture. Some Frick descendants still have keys to this mod-est *pied à terre*, which, as well as what you see, has a bowling alley in the basement.

HIGHLIGHTS

- *The Progress of Love*, Fragonard
- *Mall in St James's Park*, Gainsborough
- *Sir Thomas More*, Holbein
- *Officer and the Laughing Girl*, Vermeer
- *The Polish Rider*, Rembrandt
- *Virgin and Child with Saints*, Van Eyck
- *Lady Meux*, Whistler
- *Philip IV of Spain*, Velázquez
- The Russell Page garden

INFORMATION

- ✚ F4
- ✉ 1 E70th St
- ☎ 212/288 0700
- 🕐 Tue–Sat 10–6, Sun 1–6. Closed holidays
- 🍴 None
- 🚇 6 68th St
- 🚌 M1, M2, M3, M4
- ♿ Good
- 💲 Cheap
- ↔ Central Park (➤ 40)
- ❓ Lectures, Wed 5.30PM

Virgin and Child with Saints, *Van Eyck*

19

WHITNEY MUSEUM OF AMERICAN ART

HIGHLIGHTS

- The Biennial
- *Circus*, Alexander Calder
- The Hoppers
- The O'Keeffes
- *Dempsey and Firpo*, George Bellows
- The Louise Nevelsons
- The drawbridge

INFORMATION

- ✚ F3
- ✉ 945 Madison Ave
- ☎ 212/570 3600
- 🕐 Wed, Fri–Sun 11–6, Thu 1–8. Closed holidays
- 🍴 Café
- 🚇 6 77th St
- 🚌 M1, M2, M3, M4
- ♿ Good
- 💲 Moderate
- ❓ Lectures, video/film
  Whitney at the Philip Morris Building (✉ Park Ave at 42nd St, ☎ 212/878 2550. 🕐 Mon–Fri 11–6. Closed holidays)

"More modern than the Modern, the Whitney wants to be as unpredictable as the artist du jour, and very often succeeds. It's a New York tradition to sneer at the Biennial, whether or not one has seen the show."

No room at the Met Sculptor and patron of her contemporaries' work, Gertrude Vanderbilt Whitney offered her collection to the Met in 1929, but the great institution turned up its nose, and Whitney was forced to found the Whitney. In 1966, Marcel Breuer's cantilevered, granite-clad Brutalist block was completed to house it in suitably controversial manner, and here it lours still, not universally loved, but impossible to overlook. The Whitney's core collection now reads like a roll-call of the American (and immigrant) greats from earlier this century – Edward Hopper, Thomas Hart Benton, Willem de Kooning, Georgia O'Keeffe, Claes Oldenburg, Jasper Johns, George Bellows, Jackson Pollock are a few (the male to female ratio has improved, but barely). Let's hope the curators and buyers are as good as Gertrude at spotting talent for the future. There are so many more artists these days ...

Lucky dip From the important and delicious collections, work is plucked and hung, oftentimes emphasising a single artist's work, other times proving more eclectic. There's an active Film and Video department, and two branches. There used to be four branches in Manhattan alone during the art boomtime of the 1980s. The Whitney Biennial (in the spring of odd-numbered years) provides an echo of those days, when the New York art pack gets sweaty debating the merits and demerits of the chosen few on show and of the curator's vision – for the Biennial is invitational, and makes careers.

AMERICAN MUSEUM OF NATURAL HISTORY

❝Partly a lovable anachronism, this 125-year-old hulk is stuffed with dinosaur skeletons to pacify bawling brats, but the best things are the blue whale's cocktail bar and the low-tech dioramas. Don't change a thing.**❞**

Who's who Of the 36 million things owned by the Museum – which is, needless to say, the largest such institution in the world – only a small percentage is on show. The museum does happen to be changing, actually, with a $45-million cash injection going mostly into the buildings themselves, cleaning up windows and revealing original features. The Fourth Floor, where all vertebrate fossils, including dinosaurs, are, reopens in two stages, with the partially interactive dinosaurs having come online by now. There's far too much to see in one day, with three city blocks and the entire evolution of life on earth covered. Not-to-be-missed items include the Barosaurus rearing up to her full 55 feet to protect her young from a T-rex attack – and, on the first floor, the 94-foot blue whale dominating the two-storey Hall of Ocean Life and Biology of Fishes and presiding over its own bar.

More gems Another highlight is the 563-carat Star of India blue star sapphire, part of the unbelievable Hall of Meteorites, Minerals and Gems, containing almost $50m worth of precious stones, plus the 34-ton Ahnighito meteorite. The cutest part of the museum, though, is where animals of all sizes are displayed behind glass in *tableaux vivants* (or *tableaux morts*) of considerable artistic merit. Adjoining sub-museums are the astronomy department's Hayden Planetarium, containing the Guggenheim Space Theater and the Sky Theater; and the Nature Max theatre, where a four-storey screen shows ecological blockbusters.

HIGHLIGHTS

- Blue whale
- Barosaurus
- Herd of stuffed elephants
- New dinosaur halls
- Hall of Human Biology and Evolution
- Sky Shows at the Planetarium
- Star of India
- The dioramas
- Dinosaur embryo
- The 'Diner Saurus' (fast food)

INFORMATION

- ➕ E2
- ✉ Central Park West at 79th St
- ☎ 212/769 5100
- ◷ Mon–Thur, Sun 10–5:45; Fri–Sat 10–8:45
- 🍴 Three
- Ⓜ B, C 81st St
- 🚌 M7, M10, M11, M79
- ♿ Good
- ⊞ Moderate
- ↔ Central Park (40), Lincoln Center (39)
- ❓ 75min tours until 3:15PM Hayden Planetarium (☎ 212/769 5920)

The barosaurus

21

METROPOLITAN MUSEUM OF ART

HIGHLIGHTS

- Temple of Dendur
- Period rooms, American Wing
- *Diptych*, Van Eyck
- *Young Woman with a Water Jug*, Vermeer
- *Venus and Adonis*, Rubens
- *Grand Canal, Venice*, Turner
- *Sunflowers*, Van Gogh
- *Madame X*, Sargent
- Rooftop Sculpture Garden

The Great Hall

INFORMATION

- ✚ F3
- ✉ 1000 Fifth Ave, 82nd St
- ☎ 212/535 7710
- ◉ Tue, Wed, Sun 9:30–5:15; Fri, Sat 9:30–8.45. Closed 25 Dec, 1 Jan
- 🍴 Cafeteria, restaurant, bar
- 🚇 4, 5, 6 86th St
- 🚌 M1, M2, M3, M4
- ♿ Very good
- 💲 Moderate
- ↔ Central Park (➤40), Whitney (➤42), Guggenheim (➤45)
- ❓ The Cloisters (➤48) houses more of the Met's medieval collections. Same-day admission on Met ticket.

❝*It'll give you bigger blisters than the Uffizi, bigger chills than the Sistine Chapel, and take a bigger slice of vacation time than all dinners. It's so big, it doesn't just contain Egyptian artefacts, but an entire Egyptian building.*❞

Art city The limestone Beaux-Arts façade with its tremendous steps was a 1902 addition to the Calvert Vaux (of Central Park fame) red-brick Gothic building buried inside here. There are several more building-within-buildings, interior gardens and courtyards, such is the scale of the Met. The 15BC Temple of Dendur, in its glass-walled bemoated chamber east of the main entrance on the first floor (which Americans view as the second), is the best known, but there's also the Astor Court above it – a replica Ming dynasty scholar's courtyard – plus, in the American Wing, a score of period rooms, and the vast and sunlit garden court with its hodgepodge of Tiffany glass and topiary, a Frank Lloyd Wright window and the entire Federal-style façade of the United States Bank from Wall Street.

Where to start? How to stop? A quarter of the 3 million-plus objects are up at any one time, so, pace yourself. Relax. There are about 15 discrete collections. Some visitors decide on one or two per visit – 13th–18th-century European Paintings (or part thereof), and Ancient Art, perhaps – and leave it at that. Or you could structure a route around one or two favourite and familiar works. The Information Center in the ground ('first') floor Uris Center, with its Orientation Theater and giant floor plans, is the place to begin, whatever you decide to see. Consider visiting on Friday or Saturday evening, when a string quartet serenades you, and the crowds are often thinner.

SOLOMON R GUGGENHEIM MUSEUM

> **"***If you could just happen across Frank Lloyd Wright's space-age rotunda, your eyes would pop out of their sockets, but it's the planet's best-known modern building, so you are prepared. Don't forget the museum inside.***"**

Museum of architecture This is the great Frank Lloyd Wright's only New York building, his 'Pantheon', as he called it. It was commissioned by Solomon R at the urging of his longtime friend and taste tutor, Baroness Hilla Rebay von Ehrenwiesen, though the incredibly wealthy metal-mining magnate died ten years before it was completed in 1959. The giant white nautilus is certainly arresting, but it's the interior that unleashes the most superlatives. Take the elevator up, and snake the quarter mile down the ramp to see why.

Museum of art There are something like 6,000 pieces in the Guggenheim Foundation's possession. Solomon R and his wife Irene Rothschild abandoned the Old Masters they sought at first, when Hilla Rebay introduced them to Kandinsky, Mondrian and Moholy-Nagy, Léger, Chagall and Gleizes, and they got hooked on the moderns. See also the early Picassos in the small rotunda and the 1992 tower extension, and, if you like the Impressionists and Post-Impressionists, then look for the Thanhauser Collection, donated to the museum by art dealer Joseph K Thanhauser and always on display – unlike the Guggenheim holdings, which are rotated.

Branch museum If you want more art, the downtown SoHo 'branch' of the Gugg (✉ 575 Broadway; ☎ 212/423-3600) opened in 1992, showing one or two temporary exhibitions per year, as well as some more from the collections.

HIGHLIGHTS

- The building
- *L'Hermitage à Pontoise,* Pissarro
- *Paris Through the Window,* Chagall
- *Woman Ironing,* Picasso
- *Nude,* Modigliani
- Kandinskys
- Klees
- Légers
- Downtown Guggenheim
- The shop

INFORMATION

- ✚ G2
- ✉ 1071 Fifth Ave at 88th St
- ☎ 212/423 3500
- 🕐 Fri–Wed 10–8. Closed 25 Dec, 1 Jan, Thu
- 🍴 Café
- Ⓜ 4, 5, 6 86th St
- 🚌 M1, M2, M3, M4
- ♿ Very good
- 💲 Moderate
- ↔ Whitney (➤42), Metropolitan Museum of Art (➤44), Central Park (➤40)
- ❓ Lecture programme

COOPER-HEWITT MUSEUM OF DESIGN

HIGHLIGHTS

- Panelling in the hall
- Solarium
- Garden
- Architectural drawings
- Summer concerts
- Textiles
- Exhibitions

INFORMATION

- ✚ G2
- ✉ 2 E91st St
- ☎ 212/860 6868
- ⊕ Tue–Sat 10–5 (Tue till 9pm), Sun noon–5. Closed holidays
- 🍴 None
- Ⓢ 4, 5, 6 86th St
- 🚌 M1, M2, M3, M4
- 🖕 Good
- 🔲 Cheap
- ↔ Central Park (➤ 40), Guggenheim (➤ 45)
- ❓ Tours available

Top: the former residence of the industrialist Andrew Carnegie, now home to the Cooper-Hewitt Museum

"*The charming National Museum of Design collections are, Frick-like, housed in an equally charming, wood-panelled mansion. When snow falls in the holiday season, there's nowhere better to indulge in mawkishly nostalgic reveries.*"

Carnegie-Hewitt The mansion belonged to industrialist Andrew Carnegie, who, in 1903, had asked architects Babb, Cook & Willard for 'the most modest, plainest, and most roomy house in New York City'. This he did not receive (apart from the roominess), since this little château was built with mod cons galore – central heating, air conditioning, elevators – and a big gated garden to keep out the squatter neighbours. The entire neighbourhood came to be known as Carnegie Hill, thanks to his early patronage. Andrew's wife, Louise, lived here till her death in 1946, then, some 20 years later, the Carnegie Corporation donated it to the Smithsonian Institution to house the Hewitt sisters' collections. Still following? The three sisters, Amy, Eleanor and Sarah, had become infatuated with the V&A on a visit to London in 1897, and this had set them off on their lifelong collecting spree.

And Cooper The girls' grandpa was Peter Cooper, founder of the Cooper Union college of art and architecture, and he offered the collection a home there, where it stayed until 1967. The contemporary Cooper-Hewitt is a vibrant institution where all manner of events are laid on. In addition to the collections, some of which are on display (though it's hard to predict which), there are various reference resources here, including the country's biggest architectural drawings collection, a textile library with a 3,000-year span, auction catalogues, wallpapers, jewellery, earthenware – you name it.

YANKEE STADIUM

❝*Final out, bottom of the Ninth and, whether the home team won or lost, Sinatra's* New York, New York *wafts over the blue seats. Baseball (which is deeply troubled) embodies the American spirit – this stadium is New York.*❞

What does baseball mean? New Yorkers are about as keen on sports as the Pope is on Catholicism, even though a team nowadays is almost more a brand name than a unit of athletes. Professional baseball today is a big bucks business, which reached its apogee of heartlessness in 1994, when the players went on strike against a proposed salary cap. To Yankee fans – already licking wounds inflicted by unpopular team owner, George Steinbrenner – this signalled the end of baseball, and thus of America.

The house that Ruth built If you want to see what makes the New York heart tick (unless it belongs to a fan of the 1962 upstart National League NY Mets), go see a Yankees home game. The Yankees dominated the early eras of baseball. In 1920, George Herman 'Babe' Ruth joined the team and quickly became a hero of such mythic stature that his popularity built them a stadium in 1923 (renovated in the mid-1970s).

Where have you gone, Joe Di Maggio? The Babe's No 3 is only one of the 'retired' numbers, which honour great players who bore them, and will never be re-allocated. Lou Gehrig was No 4 (killed by a disease, that they named after him); No 5 was Joe Di Maggio's (he married Marilyn Monroe and pulled off a 56-game hitting streak); No 7 was Mickey Mantle's, and No 8 was Yogi Berra's. These four played between 1946 and 1960, when the team won eight World Series titles; they are why Yankee fans 'bleed pinstripes'.

HIGHLIGHTS

- Don Mattingly
- Bleachers bums (cheap seats)
- 7th Inning Stretch (mid-game break for spectators)
- Eddie Layton, organist
- 'Giveaway Days'

INFORMATION

- ✚ Off I2
- ✉ E 161st St, Bronx
- ☎ 718/293 4300; Ticketmaster 212/307 1212
- ◷ Season runs Apr–Oct; check schedule for home games
- 🍴 Concession stands
- Ⓜ 4, D, C (weekdays) 161st St
- 🚌 BX6, BX13, BX55
- ♿ Good
- 💰 Expensive

THE CLOISTERS

HIGHLIGHTS

- Unicorn Tapestries
- Fuentidueña Chapel
- Cuxa Cloister
- Saint Guilhem Cloister
- Annunciation Altarpiece
- Boppard stained glass
- Rosary bead carved with the Passion
- Bonnefont Cloister herb garden
- Ramparts – views to Hudson

INFORMATION

- ✚ Off F1
- ✉ Fort Tryon Park, Bronx
- ☎ 718/923 3700
- ◷ Tue–Sun 9:30–4.45 (Mar–Oct till 5:15PM). Closed holidays
- Ⓢ A 190th St
- ▣ M4
- ♿ Good
- 📷 Moderate
- ❓ Tours: Tue–Fri 3PM, Sun noon. Joint same-day admission with the Met. The Cloisters offers a concert programme of live and recorded medieval music

❝What is this 12th-century Spanish apse attatched to a Romanesque cloister and a Gothic chapel doing in the Bronx? The hallucinogenic incongruity of the Met's medieval branch would be its trump, but for its heavenly sights. ❞

Medieval-world The building in Fort Tryon Park – a site in the far north of Manhattan Island that was donated by Rockefeller Jr – is not medieval, you'll be astonished to learn, but there are plenty of parts of buildings inside it that are. The 12th-century pink stone Cuxa Cloister was liberated from the French Pyrenees, and the 3,000 limestone blocks of the Fuentidueña Chapel apse were rescued from the ruins of the church of Saint-Martín in Spain. The Cloisters are not some Disney-esque simulacrum of medieval Europe, however. Being able to gaze at the ribbed vaulting of the late-Romanesque Pontaut Chapter House, or strolling past the early-Flemish Annunciation Altarpiece of Robert Campin to the familiar 15th-century Unicorn Tapestries are treats that have not been possible in Europe since the Age of Chivalry exhibition at London's Royal Academy gathered together high points of medieval art some years ago.

Through the ages The collections are arranged chronologically, so that one can trace not only the metamorphosis of architectural styles, but also of the medieval mind – by turns awestruck, playful, bawdy and terrified. The bulk of the art and architecture was amassed by sculptor George Gray Bernard early this century. Much was rescued from ruin – the effigy of the Crusader, Jean d'Alluye, for instance, was doing duty as a bridge, while the priceless Unicorn Tapestries were once draped over fruit trees as frost blankets.

NEW YORK's *best*

BUILDINGS

Reach for the sky

The tallest building in the world is the Sears Roebuck Tower in Chicago, but, in their day, these New York structures were the highest: Park Row Building (✉ 15 Park Row, 1899–1908, 386ft), Chrysler Building (1929–1930, 1,048ft), Empire State Building (1930–1972, 1,250ft), World Trade Center Towers (1972–79, 1,350ft). Contrary to popular myth the Flatiron was never the tallest.

CATHEDRAL OF ST JOHN THE DIVINE
Started in 1892, and not finished yet, this would be the world's biggest.
🚇 Off G1 ✉ Amsterdam Ave, W112th St ☎ 212/316 7540
🕐 Mon–Sat 7AM–5PM, Sun 7AM–8PM 🚇 1, 9 110st St

CITICORP CENTER
The 45-degree lightbox is one of the skyline's greatest hits at night. The four-legged base shelters St Peter's Church and the great atrium.
🚇 F6 ✉ 153 E53rd St 🚇 6 51st St

The Lower Manhattan skyline, dominated by the twin towers of the World Trade Center

THE DAKOTA
First of the great Upper West Side luxury apartment blocks, designed by Henry Hardenbergh, but famous as John Lennon's murder site.
🚇 E3 ✉ 1 W72nd St, Central Park West 🚇 B, C 72nd St

FLATIRON BUILDING
Named after its amazing shape – an isosceles triangle with a sharp angle pointing uptown – this 1902 skyscraper is a universal hit.
D8 175 Fifth Ave, E22–23rd streets N, R 23rd St

LEVER HOUSE
See the birth of the city – the Seagram, and this 1952 Skidmore, Owings & Merrill Corbusian were twin precursors of all glass blocks.
E5 390 Park Ave, 53–54th streets 212/960 4685
Lobby Mon–Fri 10–5, Sun 1–5 E, F Fifth Ave

'LIPSTICK BUILDING'
This likeable 1986 show-off is by John Burgee with Philip Johnson.
F5 885 Third Ave, 55–56th streets 6 51st St

METLIFE BUILDING
Known to New Yorkers as the Pan Am Building – which it was until 1981 – it's by Bauhaus priest Walter Gropius, plus Emery Roth & Sons and Pietro Belluschi, and was hated for blocking the Park Avenue vista.
E6 200 Park Ave, 44–45th streets 4, 5, 6, 7 42nd St

NY STOCK EXCHANGE
Neo-classical façade dates only from 1903. See trading from the gallery and recall the Crash of '29 that heralded the Depression.
A13 20 Broad St 212/656 5167 Mon–Fri 9:15–4
2, 3, 4, 5 Wall St; 1, 9 Rector St; J, M, Z Broad St Free

SEAGRAM BUILDING
Mies van der Rohe's 1958 bronze glazed tower is *the* Modernist landmark. Philip Johnson interiors include power-lunch Four Seasons restaurant.
E5/6 375 Park Ave, 52–53rd streets 212/572 7000
Tour 3PM Tue Two E, F Fifth Ave Free

TRUMP TOWER
The adjective 'glitzy' captured in pink marble and glass. To the 1980s!
E5 725 Fifth Ave, 56th St 212/832 2000 8AM–10PM
Several E, F Fifth Ave Free

UNITED NATIONS HEADQUARTERS
Officially outside the USA, this vast 1947–63 complex included Le Corbusier among its architects. See the lobby, or do a tour.
F6/7 First Ave at 45th St 212/963 7713 Daily 9:15–4:45, closed weekends Jan–Feb, 1 Jan, 25 Dec, Thu Café and restaurant 4, 5, 6, 7 42nd St, Grand Central Free

WORLD FINANCIAL CENTER
Cesar Pelli's waterfront World Trade Center neighbour includes the fab Winter Garden atrium, with palm trees, plus marina and piazza.
A12 200 Liberty St 212/945 0505 Many 1, 9, N, R Cortlandt St; A, C, E Chambers St; 4, 5 Fulton St Free

The Flatiron Building was one of the first structures to be erected around a steel frame

OF THE OLD

> See Top 25 Sights for
> **FRICK MANSION ➤41**
> **SCHERMERHORN ROW,**
>   **SOUTH STREET SEAPORT ➤27**

St Patrick's Cathedral

Literary New York

Old New York is the title of a collection of Edith Wharton novellas that brings to life the *Age of Innocence* (the Wharton novel, filmed by Scorsese). The other chronicler of 19th-century New York manners was, of course, Henry James, especially in *Washington Square* (filmed as *The Heiress*). For the jazz age of the 1920s, read F Scott Fitzgerald's short stories.

BLOCK BEAUTIFUL

This picturesque, tree-lined 1920s row really is called this. Also see the pretty square near by, centred on private Gramercy Park (➤54).
➕ D8 ⊠ E19th St, Irving Place/ Third Ave 🚇 N, R 14th St Union Square; 6 23rd St

CITY HALL

A French Renaissance-style façade and an elegant Georgian interior – see it by visiting the Governor's room, with small furniture museum.
➕ B12 ⊠ Broadway at Murray St ☎ 212/788 3000 🕐 Mon–Fri 10–3:30 🚇 2, 3 Park Place; 4, 5, 6 Brooklyn Bridge/City Hall; N, R City Hall 🎟 Free

SINGER BUILDING & HAUGHWOUT STORE

Two of the best ambassadors for the SoHo Cast Iron Historic District (➤54) – the 26 blocks of skyscraper forerunners, now galleries and posh boutiques. The Haughwout had the first Otis steam elevator.
➕ C10 ⊠ 561 and 488 Broadway 🚇 N, R Prince St; B, D, F, Q Broadway/Lafayette

ST PATRICK'S CATHEDRAL

James Renwick's Gothic Revival cathedral is the US's biggest for Catholics.
➕ E5/6 ⊠ Fifth Ave at 50th St ☎ 212/753 2261 🕐 6AM–9PM 🚇 6 51st St; E, F Fifth Ave 🎟 Free

WASHINGTON SQUARE – 'THE ROW' AND ARCH

'The Row' (1–13, North side) housed movers and shakers of early 19th-century New York city – read Henry James's *Washington Square* for details.
➕ C9 ⊠ South end of Fifth Ave 🚇 N, R 8th St; A, C, E, B, D, F, Q W4th St

WOOLWORTH BUILDING

The world's tallest until the Chrysler, Cass Gilbert's Gothic beauty has NYC's richest lobby – see witty bas reliefs of architect and tycoon.
➕ B12 ⊠ 233 Broadway 🕐 Lobby hours, Mon–Fri 7–6. Closed holidays 🚇 2, 3 Park Place; N, R City Hall

VIEWS

BROOKLYN HEIGHTS ESPLANADE

As traffic clogs the BQE (the Brooklyn–Queens Expressway) beneath your feet, all is serene on this elegantissimo promenade, with some of New York's most covetable houses and very rare gardens at your back and Manhattan's financial centre spread out before you.

🚇 Off C14 ✉ West End of Clark St 🚉 2, 3 Clark St

WORLD FINANCIAL CENTER (►51)

Join the Wall Street hordes in the piazza for sunset over the Hudson.

ROOSEVELT ISLAND TRAMWAY

One of New York City's oddities is this Swiss-made cable car that has been flying passengers to the site of the NYC Lunatic Asylum (undergoing restoration) and on into Queens since 1976.

🚇 F5 ✉ Second Ave, 60th St ☎ 212/832 4543 🕐 Mon–Fri 6AM–2AM, weekends 6AM–3AM 🚉 B, Q Lexington Ave 💰 Cheap

STATEN ISLAND FERRY

Those three words 'Staten Island Ferry' are nearly always followed by these three: 'city's best bargain'. The voyage is a tiny vacation.

🚇 A14 ✉ Whitehall Terminal ☎ 212/806 6901, 718/390 5253 🕐 24hr service 🚉 N, R Whitehall St South Ferry 💰 Cheap

PARK AVENUE FROM CARNEGIE HILL

Let your eyes sweep as far as the MetLife building – a view best experienced during the Christmas holiday season when pine trees bedecked with sparkling white lights bisect the route.

🚇 G2 🚉 6 86th St, 96th St

A table with a view

This is a sought-after commodity. Eat well too (and pay handsome sums) at Brooklyn's River Café (✉ 1 Water St ☎ 718/522 5200) or the Water's Edge in Queens (✉ 44th Drive, East River, Long Island City ☎ 718/482 0033) with its free boat taxi and floor-to-ceiling windows. The Water Club (✉ 500 E30th St ☎ 212/683 3333) has the view in the other direction and new American food. Or dine waterside on a more modest budget at the Boathouse Café (☎ 212/517 2233) on Central Park's lake.

Lower Manhattan and the East River viewed from Brooklyn Heights

NEIGHBOURHOODS

TriBeCa

The East Village

Not so much a neighbourhood as a state of mind – the one that parents hope is just a phase. At the time of writing, pierced lips, nipples, navels, etc, were *de rigueur*, and tattoos were old hat. The streets themselves are bursting with cheap and good restaurants, divey bars, coffee lounges, vintage clothing stores and wholefood emporia. Recently revived, pretty Tompkins Square Park has great concerts in summer.

> See Top 25 Sights for
> **CHINATOWN ➤ 30**
> **GREENWICH VILLAGE ➤ 31**

EAST VILLAGE
No hipper place exists. If you're over 30 and not in black, you feel odd.
➕ D/E10 🚇 F 2nd Ave; 6 Astor Place

GRAMERCY PARK AND FLATIRON
The former, peaceful and pleasant to stroll, is centred on the eponymous park; the latter on the eponymous building (➤51). It's the latest real estate label, grown out of the photography district, hangout of models, and the new Restaurant Row is Park Avenue South.
➕ D8 🚇 N, R, 6 23rd St

LITTLE ITALY
Reduced to Mulberry Street, this is really a former neighbourhood, but nice to stroll and café hop. Skip the touristy red-sauce spaghetterias, but see the Feast of San Gennaro (September), then Scorsese's *Mean Streets* for the real thing.
➕ C10/11 🚇 6 Spring St

LOWER EAST SIDE
Where the melting pot landed; birth of Jewish New York: Orchard Street.
➕ D11/ D12/ E11/E12 🚇 F Delancey St

SOHO
South of Houston (say '*How*-stun') saw 1980s art mania, when its gorgeous cast-iron framed buildings were loft-ised on the cheap. Now it's for expensive boutique shopping, weekend wandering, gallery-hopping, and posing.
➕ B/C10 🚇 N, R Prince St; C, E Spring St

THEATER/GARMENT DISTRICT
As they sound, and delineated more or less by Sixth and Ninth avenues and 34th to 59th streets, with theatres clustering on – where else? – Broadway, and the 'garmentos' – those who work in the fashion trade – along Seventh Avenue.
➕ D5/6 and C/D6 🚇 N, R, 1, 2, 3 Times Sq

TRIBECA
Like SoHo, the Flatiron and the East Village, the 'Triangle Below Canal' was designated a neighbourhood by real estate agents, but the sobriquet stuck. Once a windy wasteland of warehouses, now it has the top tables (Bouley, Nobu, Chanterelle), plus rich architects, artists and movie makers in lofts.
➕ A/B10 🚇 A, 1, 2, 3 Chambers St

MUSEUMS

Musical soirées

At major museums this is an innovation catching on happily. Among those to have jumped on the bandwagon are: the Guggenheim (uptown), with jazz in Frank Lloyd Wright's rotunda, the Metropolitan Museum of Art, which started the whole thing, and its Cloisters outpost, and the Frick, with chamber music in its beautiful courtyard.

FORBES MAGAZINE GALLERIES
Toy soldiers, Fabergé eggs, plus art.
➕ C9 ✉ 63 Fifth Ave, 12th St ☎ 212/206 5548 🕐 Tue, Wed, Fri, Sat 10–4 🚇 4, 5, 6 14th St 💲 Free

JEWISH MUSEUM
Chronicling Jewish experience world-wide, with artefacts from 4,000 years.
➕ G2 ✉ 1109 Fifth Ave ☎ 212/423 3200 🕐 Sun–Thu 11–5:45, Tue till 8PM 🍴 Café 🚇 4, 5, 6 86th St 💲 Moderate

LOWER EAST SIDE TENEMENT MUSEUM
A reconstruction of life in this 1863 tenement block, plus talks, tours, etc.
➕ D11 ✉ 97 Orchard St ☎ 212/431 0233 🕐 Tue–Fri 11–4, Sun 10–5 🚇 F, J, M, Z Delancey St; B, D, Q Grand St 💲 Cheap

NEW MUSEUM OF CONTEMPORARY ART
What MoMA stops at, Whitney shows; where Whitney balks, this starts.
➕ C10 ✉ 583 Broadway, between Houston and Prince streets ☎ 212/219 1222 🕐 Wed–Sun noon–6, Sat till 8PM 🚇 N, R Prince St 💲 Cheap

NEW YORK CITY FIRE MUSEUM
See the firefighting dog! Pretty Beaux-Arts station.
➕ B10 ✉ 278 Spring St, SoHo ☎ 212/691 1303 🕐 Tue–Sat 10–4 🚇 C, E Spring St 💲 Contribution

New York City Fire Museum

PIERPONT MORGAN LIBRARY
McKim, Mead & White's 1902 palazzo for Morgan's sublime manuscripts.
➕ D/E 7 ✉ 29 E36th St ☎ 212/685 0008 🕐 Tue–Sat 10:30–5, Sun 1–5 🚇 6 33rd St 💲 Moderate

POLICE ACADEMY MUSEUM
See Al Capone's gun and learn about Prohibition raids – maybe from a cop.
➕ D8 ✉ 235 E20th St ☎ 212/477 9753 🕐 Mon–Fri 9–3, call first 🚇 4, 5, 6 14th St 💲 Free

GALLERIES & OUTDOOR ART

Outside art

Save time – combine art with sightseeing.

Stabile (1971), Alexander Calder (A12 6 World Trade Center)

Group of Four Trees (1972), Jean Dubuffet (B12 Chase Manhattan Bank, Pine/Nassau/ Liberty streets)

Gay Liberation (1980), George Segal (B9 Christopher Park, Sheridan Square)

Prometheus (1934), Paul Manship (E5 Rockefeller Center)

Single Form (1964), Barbara Hepworth (F7 pool of Secretariat Building, UN, First Ave, 46th St)

Reclining Figure (1965), Henry Moore (D4 Reflecting Pool, Lincoln Center)

Night Presence IV (1972), Louise Nevelson (G2 Park Ave, 92nd St)

Red Cube, *by Isamu Noguchi, Church Street*

SOHO GALLERIES

Doing the SoHo galleries, brunch, and shopping (in a different order of importance) is one version of the quintessential New York Saturday. These commercial spaces show contemporary work – perhaps not as cutting edge as in the 1980s. Still, the following are major. (Call for current show.)

 Generally Tue–Sat 11–6 N, R Prince St; C, E Spring St

Dia Center for the Arts	393 W Broadway	212/925 9397
Gagosian	136 Wooster St	212/228 2878
Leo Castelli	420 W Broadway	212/431 5160
Leo Castelli II	578 Broadway	212/431 6279
Mary Boone	417 W Broadway	212/431 1818
Meisel	141 Prince St	212/677 1340
Paula Cooper	155 Wooster St	212/674 0766
Sonnabend	420 W Broadway	212/966 6160
Vorpal	459 W Broadway	212/334 3939
Ward-Nasse	178 Prince St	212/925 6951

UPTOWN GALLERIES

Different from SoHo viewing – dressier, more demanding – so we list fewer.

Fischbach	24 W57th St	212/759 2345
Gagosian	980 Madison Ave	212/744 2313
Janis	110 W57th St	212/586 0110
Marlborough	40 W57th St	212/541 4900
Pace	32 E57th St	212/421 3292

FOR KIDS

See Top 25 Sights for
AMERICAN MUSEUM OF NATURAL
HISTORY AND PLANETARIUM ➤43
CENTRAL PARK: CAROUSEL ➤40
CHINATOWN ➤30
EMPIRE STATE BUILDING ➤33
SOUTH STREET SEAPORT CRUISE ➤27
WORLD TRADE CENTER ➤28
YANKEE STADIUM ➤47

BRONX ZOO

The biggest city zoo in the US has 4,000 animals, a kid's zoo, and monorail.
➕ Off I1 ✉ Fordham Road, Bronx River Parkway Northeast
☎ 718/367 1010 🕐 Apr–Oct 10–5, Nov–Mar 10–4:30
🍴 Restaurant 🚇 2, 5 Pelham Parkway 🏷 Moderate

CHILDREN'S MUSEUM OF THE ARTS

Highlights: the Monet Ballpond, Architects Alley and the Wonder Theater.
➕ C11 ✉ 72 Spring St ☎ 212/274 0986 🕐 Tue–Sun 11–5
🚇 6 Spring St 🏷 Moderate

CHILDREN'S MUSEUM OF MANHATTAN

Ignore the word 'museum' – here they can make their own TV show.
➕ D5 ✉ 212 W83rd St ☎ 212/721 1234 🕐 Sep–May, Mon, Wed, Thu 1:30–5:30, Fri–Sun 10–5; Jun–Aug, Wed–Mon 10–5 🚇 4, 5, 6 86th St 🏷 Moderate

FAO SCHWARZ

The world's most famous toyshop – see the movie *Big*; set advance spending and time limits. The giant singing clock at the entrance is scary.
➕ E5 ✉ 767 Fifth Ave ☎ 212/644 9400 🕐 Mon–Sat 9–9, Sun 10–8 🚇 E, F Fifth Ave; 4, 6 59th St 🏷 Free

HARLEY DAVIDSON CAFÉ AND PLANET HOLLYWOOD

Two shameless pack-em-in theme canteens that ten-year-olds adore. Also check out the supermodel-owned Fashion Café in Rockefeller Centre.
➕ E5 ✉ 1370 Sixth Ave, W56th St and 140 W57th St ☎ 212/245 6000 and 212/333 7827 🕐 Daily till late 🚇 N, R, B, Q 57th St
🏷 Moderate

SERENDIPITY 3 (➤ 67)

WONDERCAMP

This vast multi-activity centre is the perfect place to leave the children while you hit the Met.
➕ D8 ✉ 27 W23rd St ☎ 212/243 1111 🕐 Sun–Thu 10–6:30, Fri, Sat 10–9 🚇 N, R, F 23rd St 🏷 Moderate

Kids' Broadway

All over town are theatrical troupes dedicated to the entertainment of youth. Try:

The Paper Bag Players
☎ 212/362 0431; winter season at Symphony Space
✉ Broadway at 95th St
☎ 212/864 6400

New York Children's Theater
✉ 250 W65th St
☎ 212/496 8009

Theaterworks/USA
✉ Broadway at 76th St
☎ 212/677 5959

Little People's Theater
✉ 39 Grove St
☎ 212/765 9540

FREE THINGS

See Top 25 Sights for
CENTRAL PARK ➤40
COOPER-HEWITT (TUE EVENING FREE) ➤46
**FULTON FISH MARKET, SOUTH STREET
 SEAPORT** ➤27
**GUGGENHEIM
 (THU 6–8PM PAY-WHAT-YOU-WISH)** ➤45
**MUSEUM OF MODERN ART
 (THU 5–9PM PAY-WHAT-YOU-WISH)** ➤38
NEW YORK PUBLIC LIBRARY ➤34

On Parade

New York loves a parade, and nobody does it more often than New Yorkers. The biggest are: St Patrick's Day Parade (✉ Fifth Ave, 44–86th streets 🕐 17 Mar); Easter Parade (✉ Fifth Ave, 44–59th streets 🕐 Easter Sun); Lesbian & Gay Pride Day Parade (✉ Fifth Ave, Columbus

Street entertainment often represents a sound return for a small investment

Circle– Washington Square 🕐 late June); Columbus Day Parade (✉ Fifth Ave, 44–86th streets 🕐 12 Oct); Halloween Parade (✉ Greenwich Village 🕐 31 Oct); Macy's Thanksgiving Day Parade (Central Park West, 79th St–Broadway, 34th St 🕐 Fourth Thu Nov).

BEING ON TV
Write in advance for free tickets to talk shows, etc.
✉ NBC, 30 Rockefeller Plaza ☎ 212/664 3056 🚇 B, D, F 47–50 St

BIG APPLE GREETERS
Volunteers who like showing off their city will take you places in NYC, free.
☎ 212/669 3602, or 8273; 48 hours notice required

BROOKLYN BOTANIC GARDEN
A 52-acre expanse of gorgeousness with plantings of herbs, roses, fragrant flora especially for the blind, and Shakespeare, kids' and Japanese gardens.
➕ Off F14 ✉ 1000 Washington Ave ☎ 718/622 4433 🕐 Apr–Sep, Tue–Fri 8–6, weekends 10–6; Oct–Mar, Tue–Fri 8–4:30, weekends 10–4:30 🍴 Café 🚇 2, 3 Eastern Parkway

BRYANT PARK
The summer evening 'walk in' movies are a new tradition; also concerts.
➕ D6 🚇 B, D, F, 42nd St

FORBES MAGAZINE GALLERIES (➤55)

NY STOCK EXCHANGE GALLERY (➤51)

SOHO GALLERY HOPPING (➤56)

STATEN ISLAND FERRY (➤53)
50¢ round-trip counts as free.

WALKING
The world's best walking city. You'll need around 2 minutes per block, and sunglasses.

WASHINGTON SQUARE (➤52)
In summer it's live theatre – literally. Genuinely funny stand-ups perform.

WORLD FINANCIAL CENTER (➤51)
The Winter Garden Atrium has events all year round.

GYMS

CRUNCH
Cyberpunk styling, gimmicks (live DJs, haircutting, heart-rate monitors), downtown attitude. Best classes: Terry Southerland's Knockout Boxing, Thighs and Gossip, Spinning – massed stationary bike riding.
🔲 D9 ✉ 54 E13th St; 404 Lafayette St ☎ 212/475 2018
🚇 N, R, 4, 6 Union Sq

EQUINOX
Everyone's goodlooking, and a fair bit of eyeing goes on – but what the heck, those bodies took *work*. Best classes: Patricia Moreno's; Michael Olajidé Jr's Aerobox. Uptown's spa has cranio-sacral massage, acupuncture, rolfing ...
🔲 D3 ✉ 897 Broadway; 344 Amsterdam Ave ☎ 212/780 9300
🚇 N, R 23rd St

SOHO TRAINING
A respite from the super-clubs, this is human-sized, with personal trainers that don't cost the earth, and a boxing ring. Best classes: Phil Nurse's Muay Thai, Luke Massy's Mad Dog Circuit.
🔲 C10 ✉ SoHo Building, 110 Greene St ☎ 212/219 2018
🚇 N, R Prince St

WORLD
Half spiritual haven, half professional iron-pumper's heaven – it's light and spacious, and it's open 24 hours. Best classes: You & Me Yoga (doubles isn't just tennis), NIA (Neuro-Muscular Integrative Action – don't ask), Breathe!.
🔲 D3 ✉ 1926 Broadway ☎ 212/874 0942 🚇 1, 2, 3, 9 66th St

NEW CLUBS
Of the many that were about to open at press time these are the most exciting.

CHELSEA PIERS SPORTS CENTRE
Egalitarian, vast, packed with: four-tier golf range, two ice-skating rinks, marina, climbing wall, track and field arena, big swimming pool.
🔲 B7 ✉ Piers 59–62 West Side Highway 🚇 C, E, 23rd St

REEBOK SPORTS CLUB NY
Has everything, from ski and windsurfing simulators, to fancy bistro.
🔲 D4 ✉ Near Lincoln Center
🚇 1, 2, 3, 9 66th St

Where do you work out?
Many of the things people did during the 1980s at frenetic all-night dance clubs – ie meet, sweat, schmooze, pose – are now accomplished at the gym. All New Yorkers have gym membership. Most use it. 'Where do you work out?' is a perfectly reasonable question, as unsurprising as the sight of people bouncing rhythmically in upstairs windows.

The New York gym provides more than just exercise, it's a way of life

'ONLY IN NEW YORK'

Macy's Thanksgiving Day Parade

BARNEY'S WAREHOUSE SALE

Warehouse sales are known elsewhere, but you must understand, Barney's is *the* store where every single New Yorker bar none aspires to shop for clothes. Consequently, *everyone* goes to this event. It is a zoo.

✠ C8 ✉ 255 W17th St ⏱ Feb, Sep
🚇 1, 9 18th St

BASKETBALL STARS ON THE STREET

At 'The Cage', you can see basketball played by *future* stars, as good as the pros (and it's free).

✠ B10 ✉ Sixth Ave, W3rd St 🚇 A, B, C, D, E, F W4th St

GRAND MARCH OF THE DACHSHUNDS

This is the climax of the two-hour Dachshund Octoberfest (usually the third Saturday at noon). The short-legged dogs parade around the fountain.

✠ C9 ✉ Washington Square Park
🚇 N, R 8th St

MACY'S THANKSGIVING DAY PARADE BALLOON INFLATION

Macy's Thanksgiving Day Parade (fourth Thursday in November) is fine, but better are the impromptu street parties that convene the night before, as the balloons go up.

✠ E2 ✉ Central Park West around 81st St
🚇 C 81st St

POETRY SLAMS

These are competitive poetry readings. One night a week (Friday is normal), writers declaim, chant, even sing their work to raucous crowds.

✠ D10 ✉ Nuyorican Poets Café, 236 E3rd St, Ave B-C ☎ 212/505 8183 🚇 F 2nd Ave

Wigstock

This fab Labor Day fest is as it sounds – an excuse to wear wild wigs, wild drag, and dish. RuPaul started here. Started in 1984, it has now outgrown its venue.

RUSSIAN BATHS

This has been here forever, and looks that way in the Stone Room, hot as hell, where you get your schwitze – a beating with soapy oak leaves.

✠ D10 ✉ 268 E10th St ☎ 212/473 8806 🚇 6 Astor Place

HOWARD STERN

If he didn't invent the genre of 'shock jock', this irritating, self-consciously controversial individual certainly popularised it. To hear him, tune into 92.3FM WXRK, Mon–Fri mornings.

NEW YORK
where to...

NEIGHBOURHOOD FAVOURITES

The restaurants on the following pages are in three price categories:

£££   over $50 per person

££   up to $40 per person

£   up to $25 per person

Spoilt for choice?

In a city with 17,000 restaurants, there's no need for anyone to share anyone else's preferences, even if they inhabit the same block. All New Yorkers are restaurant experts, because all New Yorkers eat out more often than in (and eating is usually means ordering in). They throw dinner parties at restaurants, and they eat alone with a book at the best tables, and their repertoire includes options for both. Listings can never do justice to the depth of choice in this town.

BRASSERIE (£–££)

The best features of this utterly *faux*-French, um, brasserie are that it's in the Mies van der Rohe Seagram Building, which is in a part of midtown not rich in options, that it is dependable, inexpensive, and never closed.

🚇 F6 ✉ 100 E53rd St (Park/Lexington Ave) ☎ 212/751 4840 🕐 Open 24 hours 🚇 6 51st St

EMPIRE DINER (£–££)

Deep in Chelsea near the river is this metallic ultra-diner (though it's candle – not neon-lit), serving meat-loaf, sandwiches, pies, salads to an assortment of types, mostly trendy.

🚇 B7 ✉ 210 Tenth Ave (22nd St) ☎ 212/243 2736 🕐 Open 24 hours 🚇 C, E 23rd St

EL TEDDY'S (£–££)

The actual-size Statue of Liberty crown on the awning, the crazy-colour mosaics, the premium margaritas, shaken not blenderised – these mark out El Teddy's from the Mexican pack, as does the menu's verve (no heart-burn burritos). Crazed with drinky office refugees at weekends.

🚇 B11 ✉ 219 W Broadway (White St) ☎ 212/941 7070 🕐 Daily till late 🚇 1, 9 Franklin St

JERRY'S (£–££)

Looking like the diner of your dreams in red naughahyde, zebra stripes and spotlights, this SoHo haunt serves comfort dishes like half a roast chicken with garlic mash, roast veggies, pastas, salads. Upper West branch mimics the downtown cool.

🚇 C10 ✉ 101 Prince St (Greene/Mercer St) ☎ 212/966 9464 ✉ 302 Columbus Ave (74–5 streets) ☎ 212/501 7500 🕐 SoHo closed Sunday evening 🚇 N, R Prince St

FANELLI'S (£)

Dear tin-ceilinged, yellowing, draughty Fanelli's is the neighbourhood bar-restaurant all neighbourhoods should include. Notice how, despite being well over a century old, it fails to charge a premium for the seasoning of history – not that it ought for these homely dishes (pasta, chilli, sandwiches, a prize burger) and this brusque service.

🚇 C10 ✉ 94 Prince St (Mercer St) ☎ 212/226 9412 🕐 Daily, 10–late 🚇 N, R Prince St

ODEON (£–££)

Arty people in this art deco TriBeCa space relax when fed with simple American-Parisian brasserie dishes – oyster fritters, blackened salmon with tomatillo sauce, grilled lamb shanks, profiteroles. This has weathered fashion.

🚇 B11 ✉ 145 W Broadway (Thomas St) ☎ 212/233 0507 🕐 Daily till late 🚇 1, 2, 3 Chambers St

O'NEALS' (£–££)

So convenient for the Lincoln Center, though the eating's patchy: black bean soup, seared spicy shrimp is the tenor of the menu, but burgers are best.

🚇 D4 ✉ 49 W64th St (Broadway) ☎ 212/787 4663 🕐 Daily till late 🚇 1, 2, 3, 9 66 St

NEW YORK SWANK

FOUR SEASONS (£££)
In the 1980s your secretary would have called weeks ahead to ensure your lunch banquette in the Grill Room here; nowadays you might instead take advantage of the 'Grill at Night' deal, where the notable Philip Johnson interior (this is in the Seagram Building) becomes an affordable sight. However, the Pool Room is a finer sight, and is the place to be at night, so you can't win, unless you pay up. Food is state-of-the-art American-trendy, using things like mahi-mahi (meaty white fish), verjus (vine by-product), and named chilis, but all in the appropriate season. Superficial décor changes four times a year.
✚ E6 ✉ 99 E52nd St (Park/Lexington Ave) ☎ 212/754 9494 🕔 Closed Sun, Sat lunch 🚇 6 51st St

LE CIRQUE (£££)
Va-airy different from Lutèce, here you come not to have a high-profile, private experience, but to be fêted by waiters, dazzled by yourselves, and to ogle other tables of maybe models, maybe power brokers, maybe Hollywooders. Owner, Sirio Maccioni, wields more glamour than his chef, Sylvain Portay, who offers the *foie gras* style, finished with compulsory crème brûlée.
✚ F4 ✉ Mayfair Hotel, 58 E65th St (Madison/Park Ave) ☎ 212/794 9292 🕔 Closed Sun 🚇 6 68th St

LES CÉLÉBRITÉS (£££)
In the sophisticated Essex House hotel is a restaurant so pretty it's like eating inside a Fabergé egg from the Forbes Galleries, except that this egg's hung with art by célébrités like James Dean. But everyone agrees how the exquisite cuisine of Christian Delouvrier is the biggest celebrity, and presented in such beautiful ways too – spun sugar shapes, seafood shells, sauce paintings, etc.
✚ E5 ✉ 155 W58th St (Sixth/Seventh Ave) ☎ 212/484 5113 🕔 Tue–Sat, dinner 🚇 N, R 57th St

LUTÈCE (£££)
Even after 30-plus years, even after being sold to a restaurant group, it still offers classic French cooking at its best. Onion tart, saddle of rabbit with wild mushrooms, tarte tatin can be ordered – satisfying and unpretentious, like the non-snob atmosphere.
✚ F6 ✉ 249 E50th St (Second/Third Ave) ☎ 212/752 2225 🕔 Closed Mon, Sat lunch, Sun 🚇 6 51st St

RIVER CAFÉ (£££)
If you can tear your eyes from the Lower Manhattan skyline beaming through the picture windows, you'll find an original mind's maybe been tinkering with deliberately American ingredients on your plate, leading to, say, fruitwood-smoked salmon on a johnnycake, or something with buffalo, wild mushrooms, fresh berries... You can actually eat the view. Just order the Brooklyn Bridge made of Valrhona chocolate.
✚ C13 ✉ 1 Water St (East River) ☎ 718/522 5200 🕔 Daily 🚇 A High St

A good deal
The Four Seasons' 'Grill at Night' deal is one way to get a lot for less. Here are more: Bouley's, Daniel's, and Lutèce's set lunches; the '21' post-theatre supper; the bar menu at Union Square Café or Gramercy Tavern and the Cub Room Café; the lunch at Gotham; and – the New Yorker's favourite – the annual summer promotion whereby scores of the city's best restaurants offer a *prix fixe* for the same price as the year. During June of the millennium, lunch at Lutèce will cost $20.00.

SCENES

Noshing

Although you will probably be OK with most menus, the New York cuisine (see panel on page 64 for what constitutes this) runs so deep, you will not hit bottom in a year. We hope this will help:

Arugula Roquette; still in everything

Bagel NY's are the best: chewy bread ring, boiled before it's baked

Bialy Crusty bagel-esque roll, with toasted onion centre

Bigos Hunter's stew, based on sauerkraut and kielbasa (Polish)

Blintz Crêpe rolled round fruit, sweet cheese (Jewish)

Burrito Soft tortilla with refried beans, beef, cheese, guac, sour cream (Mexican)

Cannoli Pastry tube with sweet ricotta cream, addictive (Italian)

Cha siu bao Steamed pork buns, dim sum (Cantonese)

Challah Braided egg bread, best stuff for French toast (Jewish)

Chè ba màu Dessert of kidney beans, green jello, coconut milk (Vietnamese)

Chowder Creamy rich seafood soup; Manhattan chowder is tomato based

BELL CAFFE (£)

A mini club scene has sprouted on the western-most blocks of SoHo's Spring Street, with this eclectic, organic café serving as central hangout. The crowds meld into the jumble of assorted chairs and colours, and spill on to the cobblestones in summer.

⊞ B10 ✉ 310 Spring St (Hudson St) ☎ 212/334 2355 🕐 Daily till late 🚇 A, C Spring

BOWERY BAR (£–££)

There's always a single white-hot place which absorbs the full deck of models, fashion hags, mag eds, Eurotrash and artistes, and this – at press time – was it. By now, *they* will have moved on, so this barn-sized former gas station with forecourt garden in an unsavoury part of town will be serving its roasted veg and caesar with chicken to people fretfully seeking Naomi.

⊞ C10 ✉ 358 Bowery (4th St) ☎ 212/475 2220 🕐 Daily till late 🚇 6 Astor Place

CUB ROOM (£–£££)

Since the day it opened, this brick-walled, glass-fronted restaurant, bar and café was a magnet for a precisely defined stratum of well-heeled, good-looking, youthful professional (OK, yuppie). Ex-Lutèce sous-chef Henry Meer is in charge of the kitchen (roasted saged squab on ratatouille with white beans, soufflé for dessert).

⊞ B10 ✉ 131 Sullivan St ☎ 212/677 4100; Café ✉ 183 Prince St ☎ 212/777 0030 🕐 Daily dinner, weekends lunch 🚇 N, R Prince St

44 (££)

The joke about this Philippe Starck-designed catwalk of a restaurant in one of the city's most glam hostelries is that it's the staff canteen for Condé Nast (*Vogue* for instance) and *New Yorker* editors and their fabulous friends – only it's not a joke, because it's true. Food is balanced, leafy, exquisite.

⊞ D6 ✉ The Royalton Hotel 44 W44th St (Fifth/Sixth avenues) ☎ 212/944 8844 🕐 Daily 🚇 B, D, F 42nd St

GRAMERCY TAVERN (££–£££)

This is Danny Meyer's (of Union Square Café) second place, and it's equally good. Armani-wearing waitstaff are so nice you nearly invite them to share Tom Colicchio's seasonal East Coast food (smoked duck 'pastrami', roasted rockfish with Manila clam sauce). It looks like a fantasy farm-house owned by artists.

⊞ D8 ✉ 42 E20th St (Broadway/Park Ave) ☎ 212/477 0777 🕐 Mon–Sat dinner, Mon–Fri lunch 🚇 6 23rd St

LUCKY CHENG'S (£)

Past its first flush of attention, this East Village place, being unique, will probably continue to pack 'em in every night. The lighter-than-usual Californian-inflected Chinese food is surprisingly good considering everyone goes to Lucky Cheng's for the waitresses. They're beautiful Asian drag queens, every one.

⊞ D10 ✉ 24 First Ave (1st/2nd streets) ☎ 212/473 0516 🕐 Daily dinner 🚇 F 2nd Ave

DELI, PIZZA, BAGEL, BRUNCH

CARNEGIE DELI (£–££)

Known to have the rudest waiters, and the biggest sandwiches. It was the one in *Broadway Danny Rose*.

📍 E5 ✉ 854 Seventh Ave (54–55th streets) ☎ 212/757 2245 🕐 Closed Sat 🚇 N, R 57th St

KATZ'S DELI (£)

The fake orgasm scene in *When Harry Met Sally*; signs saying 'Send a salami to your boy in the army'; professionally rude countermen (tip for a fatter sandwich) ... It's a fun way to get your deli introduction, and an 1888 landmark.

📍 D11 ✉ 205 E Houston St (Ludlow St) ☎ 212/254 2246 🕐 Closed Sat 🚇 F 2nd Ave

LOMBARDI'S (£)

No new coal-fired pizza ovens (essential for the correct slightly charred, crisp crust) are allowed to be built in New York, so the owner of this tiny café tracked down the grandson of the original Lombardi (Gennaro, thought to have made NY's first *ever* pizza in 1905), and revived his disused one. It still makes great pies.

📍 C11 ✉ 32 Spring St (Mott St) ☎ 212/941 7994 🕐 Daily 🚇 6 Spring St

RAYS PIZZA (£)

Every pizza joint in town is called Ray's Original or Famous Original Ray's or Original Ray's Famous, except this one. Can you guess? This *is* the original Ray's – or the one with the best claim. Tables outside in summer.

📍 C11 ✉ 27 Prince St (Mott St) ☎ 212/966 1960

🕐 Closed Sun evening 🚇 6 Spring St

ROYAL CANADIAN PANCAKE HOUSE (£)

'Pancakes make people happy' says the sign, succinctly. Over 50 fillings go into the frisbee-sized monsters. (Two branches.)

📍 F6 ✉ 1004 Second Ave (53rd St) ☎ 212/980 4131 🕐 Daily 🚇 6 51st St

SARABETHS (£)

There are outposts in the Hotel Wales and the Whitney, which says something about the class of this simple wholesome food operation. It's the bakery that thrills, though.

📍 E2 ✉ 423 Amsterdam Ave (80th/81st streets) ☎ 212/496 6280 🕐 Daily 🚇 1, 9 79th St

SERENDIPITY 3 (£–££)

The ice-cream parlour you longed for as a child, filled with toys and serving desserts that block out the person opposite. Famous for the dangerous Frozen Hot Chocolate, made with 14 different imported kinds

📍 F5 ✉ 225 E60th St (Second /Third avenues) ☎ 212/ 838 3531 🕐 Daily to midnight 🚇 4, 6 39th St

SYLVIA'S (£)

Sylvia's has surpassed institution status and made it into the industry bracket, but is still the essential Harlem stop – especially for the Gospel Brunch, when the fried chicken and cornbread comes with live singers.

📍 Off H1 ✉ 328 Lennox Ave (126th/127th St) ☎ 212/996 0660 🕐 Mon–Sat 🚇 2, 3 125th St

Chili relleno Green chilli stuffed with cheese, fried in batter (Mexican)

Chirashi Assorted raw fish on sushi rice (Japanese)

Cilantro Coriander leaf; in everything

Clam sauce Red (tomatoey) or white (wine, cream) (Italian)

Deli As a cuisine: pastrami on rye, sauerkraut, Dr Brown's soda (Jewish)

Dim sum Cantonese dumplings, buns, little dishes

Egg cream Chocolate syrup, milk, carbonated water; no egg, no cream

Enchilada Like burrito, but folded and baked (Mexican)

Gyro Broiled mystery meat, in pita, with salad

Half-sours Bright green cucumbers pickled with garlic (Jewish)

Hijiki Black tendrils of seaweed, cooked (organic places; Japanese)

Kielbasa Cured, meaty, spiced pork sausage (Polish)

Knish Thin pastry, thick potato, kasha, cheese, fruit filling (Jewish)

Latte Short coffee, long hot milk – one of many permutations

Lox Smoked salmon – with cream cheese it's the best bagel filling

OUTDOORS, VIEWS, PEOPLE-WATCHING

Maki Roll of sushi rice with filling wrapped in seaweed (Japanese)

Marinara Tomato, onion, garlic, herbs – your basic red sauce (Italian)

Napoleon Layers of pastry, cream, sometimes fruit (Italian)

Pho Vietnamese soups, clear broth with beef, vegetables

Pierogi Pasta pillows of potato, meat, or cheese, boiled or fried (Polish)

Pignoli Pine nuts, or little pine-nut crusted cookies or tarts (Italian)

Pretzel New York's are soft-centred, sea-salted, sold from carts

Rugelach Tiny, buttery rolled pastries with dried fruit (Jewish)

Sashimi Just the raw fish part of sushi

Schmear Thin slick of cream cheese for bagel use (Jewish)

Sfogliatella Shell-shaped ribbed pastry, filled with sweet ricotta (Italian)

Slice Of pizza. Best in the world

Sushi Raw fish on mound of vinegared rice (Japanese)

Tamale Stuffed cornmeal roll, wrapped in corn husk and steamed (Mexican)

Verjus Wine by-product, predicted to be in everything now

BOATHOUSE CAFÉ (£–££)

The best thing to have at this Central Park zoo is the delicious lake view, but on most tables in summer can be seen the fruit and cheese platter. Once you've elbowed your way to a seat (the queuing system is flawed), you might follow suit, since the Italian menu's average.

➕ F3 ✉ East Park Drive (73rd St) ☎ 212/517 2233 🕐 Closed Dec–Feb 🚇 6 68th St

CAFFÈ DANTE (£)

Of the several Greenwich Village tiny-round-table Italians, this one is pleasing for the way you can procure a prime sidewalk position when Reggio (at 119) is full, and for superior pastries and gelati.

➕ B10 ✉ 79 MacDougal St (Bleecker St) ☎ 212/982 5275 🕐 Daily till late 🚇 A, B, C, D, E, F W4th St

METROPOLIS CAFÉ (£–££)

The narrow terrace just above street level is a great place to scope the Greenmarket hordes and spy on the self-conscious scene at the Coffee Bar across 16th Street. It's cool inside the huge, marble-lined former bank too, especially when the piano player's on, but tiny portions (of standard modern American food) detract from total pleasure.

➕ D9 ✉ 31 Union Square W (16th St) ☎ 212/675 2300 🕐 Daily 🚇 L, N, R, 4, 6 Union Sq

MIRACLE GRILL (£)

Secreted behind East Village tenements is the prettiest garden and a restaurant pitched above the neighbourhood average. Southwestern is the style – broiled fish, chicken, shrimp, fruit salsas, salads, and the best slushy frozen strawberry margaritas.

➕ D10 ✉ 112 First Ave (6th/7th streets) ☎ 212/254 2353 🕐 Daily dinner, weekends brunch 🚇 6 Astor Place

PIETRO & VANESSA (£)

The pleasant backyard garden here is very handy for SoHo shopping when you've spent all your cash and need a bargain. The red sauce Italian food's nothing special.

➕ C11 ✉ 23 Cleveland Place. (Spring St) ☎ 212/941 0286 🕐 Daily 🚇 6 Spring St

RAINBOW ROOM (£–£££)

Several options here at the View of Views run from push-the-boat-out dinner dance extravaganza at 'Rainbow & Stars' to martinis with mixed nuts at the bar.

➕ E5 ✉ GE Building, 65th Floor, 30 Rockefeller Plaza (49–50th streets) ☎ 212/632 5100 🕐 Tue–Sun dinner 🚇 B, D, F 47–50th St

TAVERN ON THE GREEN (£££)

Shamelessly, glitteringly out-of-towny (in every sense) is this fanciful fairy palace in Central Park, where every native child celebrates some rite of passage and foreigners hold PR launches. Has a promising new chef.

➕ E4 ✉ Central Park West (67th St) ☎ 212/873 3200 🕐 Daily 🚇 1, 9 66th St

ASIAN: PHO TO SUSHI

BO KY (£)
The phrase 'no frills' doesn't do justice to the ugliness of the formica interior, but the 20-odd noodle soups are restorative and delicious.
✚ C11 ✉ 80 Bayard St (Mott St) ☎ 212/406 2292.
🕐 Daily 🚇 N, R Canal St

KELLEY & PING (£)
Fake Chinatown, with styling which dispenses with the tiresome fluorescent lights in favour of hopsack, candles and bare wood, serves satisfying spicy noodly dishes to yuppie artists and Angelika movie house patrons.
✚ C10 ✉ 127 Greene St (Houston St) ☎ 212/228 1212.
🕐 Daily 🚇 B, D, F Broadway/Lafayette

KOM TANG SOOT BUL HOUSE (£)
As you can see, this Korean barbeque place would be worth patronising for its name alone, but this style of cook-at-table, red meat feasting is fun, and this Korean Row place does it well. Your hair will smell of BBQ for days.
✚ D7 ✉ 32 W32nd St (Fifth Ave) ☎ 212/947 8482
🕐 Daily 🚇 B, D, F, N, R 34th St

JAPONICA (£–££)
Long, long ago, sushi was fashionable. Nowadays, exquisite arrangements of raw fish on rice are merely one of many things to have for dinner. This classic one is the favourite of a great many people, so go off-peak. There's tempura, teriyaki and so on for the squeamish.
✚ C9 ✉ 100 University Place (12th St) ☎ 212/243 7752
🕐 Daily 🚇 N, R, 4, 6 Union Sq

NEW YORK NOODLETOWN (£)
Hong Kong in miniature. Get salt-baked soft shell crab, caramelised beef with noodles, jumbo shrimp with black pepper sauce – oh get anything, it's all good and the price of a sandwich.
✚ C11 ✉ 281/2 Bowery (Bayard St) ☎ 212/349 0923
🕐 Daily 🚇 F East Broadway

PHO PASTEUR (£)
Opposite the jailhouse, this is a most satisfying Vietnamese place, stark of décor, bright of light, but with a novella-length menu and fabulous phood. (And Nha Trang, at 87, is just as good, if this is full.)
✚ C11 ✉ 85 Baxter St (Mulberry St) ☎ 212/608 3656 🕐 Daily 🚇 N, R Canal St

SHABU-SHABU EAST (£)
Here's a way to eat Japanese that surpasses sushi for entertainment. You get a pile of veg, a plate of wafer-thin meat or fish, and each diner has its own pot of simmering stock to cook it all.
✚ F5 ✉ 235 W55th St ☎ 212/246 2808 🕐 Daily 🚇 6 51st St

TWENTY MOTT ST (£)
One of the most popular dim sum palaces that also does a mean glossily caramelised roast duck. Despite three floors, it's war here on Sundays.
✚ C12 ✉ 20 Mott St (Bowery) ☎ 212/964 0380 🕐 Daily 🚇 F East Broadway

Wasabi Virulent green, ultra hot horseradish condiment (Japanese)

Yogurt Frozen yogurt. Euphemism for ice cream

Zeppole Type of doughnut (Italian)

For the sushi connoisseur, Yama (£–££) is the best there is. Sadly, despite its absence from restaurant guides at press time, many people share this view, and the tiny place is engulfed by salivating sushi wolves, queueing for hours.
✚ D9 ✉ 49 Irving Place (17th St) ☎ 212/475 0969
🕐 Closed Sun 🚇 N, R, 4, 5, 6 14 St Union Sq

CLOTHES

More shops

Agnès B
✉ 1063 Madison Ave
☎ 212/570 9333

Armani Exchange
✉ 568 Broadway
☎ 212/431 6000

Chanel
✉ 5 E57th St
☎ 212/355 5050

Comme des Garçons
✉ 116 Wooster St
☎ 212/219 0660

Gianni Versace
✉ 817 Madison Ave
☎ 212/744 6868

Gucci
✉ 685 Fifth Ave
☎ 212/826 2600

Hermès
✉ 11 E57th St
☎ 212/751 3181

Polo/Ralph Lauren
✉ 867 Madison Ave (72nd St)
☎ 212/606 2100

Prada
✉ 45 E57th St
☎ 212/308 2332

Timberland
✉ 709 Madison Ave
☎ 212/754 0436

Yohji Yamamoto
✉ 103 Grand St
☎ 212/966 9066

WOMEN'S

ANNA SUI
This is the woman who puts out velvet flares one year, then dayglo baby doll dirndls the next. Silly clothes, but they're revered and *loved*.
✚ C10 ✉ 113 Green St
☎ 212/941 8406 Ⓜ N, R Prince St

BETSEY JOHNSON
Sometimes outrageous, always madly coloured and usually very clingy downtown dressing-up clothes.
✚ E3 ✉ 248 Columbus Ave (71st St) and 130 Thompson St
☎ 212/362 3364 Ⓜ 1, 2, 3 72nd St

J MORGAN PUETT
An unique, timeless aesthetic from this former sculptor, who hand dyes linens, silks, cottons into cloud and earth colours and makes kind of Amish shapes with them.
✚ C10 ✉ 140 Wooster St
☎ 212/677 1200 Ⓜ N, R Prince St

NICOLE MILLER
Girl-about-town Miller designs fun, fitted suits, frocks, and accessories with tongue in cheek. Fabrics and finish don't always match the price tags. (Branch in SoHo)
✚ F4 ✉ 780 Madison Ave (66th St) ☎ 212/288 9779
Ⓜ 6 77th St

MORGANE LE FAY
Liliana Ordas's floaty, yet tailored slightly theatrical dresses, jackets, separates in strong, plain colours, and natural fibres. (Branch at 151 Spring St, SoHo.)

✚ F3 ✉ 746 Madison Ave (74th St) ☎ 212/879 9700
Ⓜ 6 77th St

MEN'S

BROOKS BROTHERS
The button-down shirts and khakis, the docksiders and plaid bermudas, the blazers ... the Ivy look.
✚ E6 ✉ 346 Madison Ave (45th St) ☎ 212/682 8800
Ⓜ 4, 6 Grand Central

TODAY'S MAN
All-purpose, good-value, gigantic casual and formal wear store. Find the likes of Lauren and St Laurent among lesser labels.
✚ C8 ✉ 625 Sixth Ave
☎ 212/924 0200 Ⓜ F 23rd St

BOTH

BANANA REPUBLIC
For high street, this is quality gear, exactly half-way between Ralph Lauren and The Gap.
✚ C9 ✉ 89 Fifth Ave
☎ 212/366 4691 Ⓜ L, N, R, 4, 6 Union Sq

CANAL JEANS
T-shirt, plaid shirt, vintage frock, cut-offs, most brands of denim, plus Carhart and CAT workwear, and their own multi-hued cottons.
✚ C10 ✉ 504 Broadway (Broome St) ☎ 212/226 1130
Ⓜ N, R Prince St

CHARIVARI
One of the best small chains anywhere, stocking carefully selected mono-chrome high style, but not fashion-victim, separates. Call for branches.
✚ C8 ✉ 257 Columbus Ave (72nd St) ☎ 212/787 7272
Ⓜ 1, 2, 3 72nd St

POSH CLOTHES FOR LESS

BIG STORES

CENTURY 21
This huge department store has an annoying lack of changing rooms except in 'European Designers', which is where the Gigli, Versace, Armani, Gaultier you wanted is anyway.
✚ A12 ✉ 22 Cortlandt St ☎ 212/227 9092 Ⓜ C, E World Trade Center

DAFFY'S
'Clothing Bargains for Millionaires' is the nonsensical motto of this three-branch chain. What they mean is: Sift through acres of orange sequined polyester catsuits hoping you recognise the Jasper, even without the label. Good for casual stuff too.
✚ C8 ✉ 111 Fifth Ave ☎ 212/529 4477 Ⓜ L, N, R, 4, 6 Union Sq

WOMEN'S

ENCORE
Very close by Michael's, and similar, except that this one stocks a little menswear too. Prices at both, by the way, are not unrelated to the originals – we're talking hundreds not tens.
✚ G3 ✉ 1132 Madison Ave ☎ 212/879 2850 Ⓜ 6 77th St

KLEIN'S OF MONTICELLO
A peacock among Lower East Side pigeons, this specialises in European designers.
✚ D11 ✉ 105 Orchard St ☎ 212/966 1453 Ⓜ F Delancey St

MICHAEL'S RESALE
Being smack in the middle of spiffy Madison Avenue, you'd expect quality here, and you get it. After all, Upper East Side ladies don't touch anything without knowing its pedigree. Labels are along the Ferragamo, Ungaro, Valentino axis.
✚ G3 ✉ 2nd Floor, 1041 Madison Ave ☎ 212/737 7273 Ⓜ 6 77th St

MEN'S

MOE GINSBERG
The classic consignment (as opposed to seconds) store is very well known. There are five floors, well-trained salesmen, a tailor next door (alterations cost extra), and just about every label up to Calvin Klein, Hugo Boss, St Laurent level.
✚ C8 ✉ 162 Fifth Ave (21st St) ☎ 212/242 3482 Ⓜ L, N, R, 4, 6 Union Sq

BOTH

INA
Few showroom samples here, but many meaty and delicious slightly worn labels, since Ina has an eye. Alaïa, Versace, Beene, Karan, Mugler, Armani are usually around.
✚ C10 ✉ 101 Thompson St (Prince St) ☎ 212/941 4757 Ⓜ N, R Prince St

OUT OF OUR CLOSET
Terin Fischer's tiny, spectacular consignment store includes current season samples from designers who make fashion fans salivate: Comme, Dolce, Mugler, Yohji, Gaultier, even Chanel. How does she do it? Contacts.
✚ C8 ✉ 136 W18th St ☎ 212/633 6965 Ⓜ F 23rd St

Thrift stores

Thrift was a dirty word in the 1980s, but now that recycling is hot, so are these stores. The SoHo Salvation Army (✉ Spring St at Lafayette St) is a cult among low-budget movie art directors, but thrift shops are still thickest on the Upper East Side. The Irvington Institute (✉ Second Ave at 80th St) and Spence Chapin (✉ Third Ave at 80th St) are especially big and fruitful. Also try Cancer Care (✉ Third Ave at 83rd St), Godmothers' League (✉ Third Ave at 82nd St), Memorial Sloane-Kettering (Third Ave at 81st St) and Call Again (✉ Second Ave at 89th St). Downtown a bit are a clutch more: The Calvary/St George's (✉ 208 E16th St) in a church basement, Repeat Performance (✉ 220 E23rd St) which benefits the City Opera, and Second Time Around, next door. The biggest is Brooklyn's Domsey Warehouse (✉ 431 Kent Ave/496 Wythe Ave ☎ 718/384 6000) with bewildering acres of work clothes, military wear, denims, prom dresses, vintage stuff sorted by era, plus a department where you pay by weight.

SUPERSTORES

Bigger, better

'New Yorkers don't need another boutique', the owner of nationwide housewares store, Crate & Barrel, declared just before his 54,000 square feet of midtown Manhattan debuted in early 1995. Regardless of whether New Yorkers agree with him, since the invasion of the superstores picked up speed, they are indeed getting precious few boutiques. Will the big guys, kill the corner deli? Most think not. New Yorkers are going to spend the cash anyway, so why not keep it in the city? And why shouldn't Manhattanites enjoy the up to 45 per cent discounts the rest of the country gets from superstores? After all, the city's been through it all before, with no harm done. The last age of giant department stores – including S Klein's, Wanamaker's, McCreery's, Bonwit Teller, and Stern Brothers of Ladies' Mile – happened, spookily enough, during the closing years of last century.

BARNES & NOBLE

Who would have predicted book shopping would become sexy? This phenomenon of – well, it's hard to say of what – opened its huge Upper West Side self, complete with coffee bar, couches, and events, in 1993 and got an instant reputation as a singles cruising arena. The Sixth Avenue branch followed, then Astor Place, then Union Square. B&N itself has been around since 1873.

✚ E2 ✉ 2289 Broadway (82nd St) ☎ 212/362 8835, and branches 🚇 1, 9 79th St

BED, BATH & BEYOND

This monster was the first to colonise Chelsea along Sixth Avenue, the neighbourhood of the giants. The name says it all. Come, see, be conquered.

✚ C8 ✉ 620 Sixth Ave (19th St) ☎ 212/255 3550 🚇 F 23rd St

BRADLEES

Like a reincarnation of S Klein's-on-the-Square, crossed with the spirit of Woolworths, everything in this gigantic emporium is cheap, cheap, cheap – just like the countless gewgaw stores along adjacent 14th Street.

✚ D9 ✉ Union Square ☎ 212/673 5814 🚇 L, N, R, 4, 6 Union Sq

COMP USA

This is possibly the most useful of all for the visitor, since it undercuts everyone and sells everything – wares hard and soft, modems and CD-ROM drives and techie doodads.

✚ D7 ✉ 420 Fifth Ave (37th St) ☎ 212/764 6224 🚇 B, D, F, N, R 34th St

CRATE & BARREL

Having refreshed your wardrobe at the uptown Barney's, you can nip next door for the wardrobe itself, perhaps in cherrywood. C&B's previous 57 stores were already renowned for taste, value, variety.

✚ F5 ✉ Madison Ave (59th St) ☎ 212/308 0011 🚇 N, R 5th Ave

TODAY'S MAN (►72)

TOWER RECORDS

The downtown superstore, with its book and video arms and Outlet, is credited with revitalising the entire area of 'NoHo' (north of Houston), because it's a youth magnet.

✚ C10 ✉ 692 Broadway (4th St) ☎ 212/505 1500 🚇 B, D, F Broadway Lafayette

TOYS 'R' US

The supermarket for children.

✚ D7 ✉ 1293 Broadway (Herald Square) ☎ 212/594 8697 🚇 B, D, F, N, R 34th St

VIRGIN MEGASTORE

The British are coming. Opening soon.

✚ D6 ✉ Times Square ☎ Not yet available 🚇 N, R 42nd St

FOOD

BALDUCCI'S

The first (alphabetically speaking) of the three Manhattan grocers that are so comprehensive, so beautifully laid out, so irresistibly stocked with things you want to devour, that you could designate them food museums. This Greenwich Village one is still owned by the family who started it as a stall across the street. The Balduccis, true to their origins, put the emphasis on Italian produce and irresistible prepared dishes (oh, the anchovy tart!).

🏠 C9 ✉️ 424 Sixth Ave (9th St) ☎️ 212/673 2600 🚇 A, B, C, D, E, F W4th St

DEAN & DELUCCA

The loft-like, mosaic-tiled-floor, all-white, vast space gives centrestage to the cornucopia at this ultimate, Elysian culinary world. Every foodstuff has its own little gallery – piles of cookies; towers of spices in tiny chrome canisters; baskets of onion ficelles, rosemary focaccia, rye, 7-grain, brioches; hemp sacks of coffee from the Himalayas to Costa Rica; fresh fish, cheese, pasta, copper pans, cookbooks – *everything*.

🏠 C10 ✉️ 560 Broadway (Prince St) ☎️ 212/431 8350 🚇 N, R Prince St

GOURMET GARAGE

GG started as a wholesale outlet for baby veg/olive oil/coffee beans, etc, run by some NYC culinary networkers. Now it's where to find yellow cherry tomatoes, dried cherries, fresh clams, truffle butter, smoked duck, smoked trout, gelati, you-name-it, and it only *acts* like it's bargain-priced. Pick up the *GG Gazette* with lunch from the deli counter.

🏠 B11 ✉️ 435 Broome St (Mercer St) ☎️ 212/941 5850 🚇 N, R Prince St

RUSS & DAUGHTERS

This, being a true New York 'appetising deli', would wither and die outside the city or even many blocks north. Devotees travel blocks and blocks for the lox, the carp, smoked whitefish, pickled herrings, etc.

🏠 D11 ✉️ 179 E Houston St (Orchard St) ☎️ 212/475 4880 🚇 F 2nd Ave

YONAH SCHIMMEL

The companion piece to the Russ & Daughters, and only a few blocks west, this remarkable, scrappy-looking anachronism is always said to serve the best fruit, cheese, kasha, and potato knishes in New York (therefore in the world).

🏠 D11 ✉️ 137 E Houston St ☎️ 212/477 2858 🚇 F 2nd Ave

ZABAR'S

This is the zaftig, wisecracking Noo Yawker of the three food heavens, just as big and bustling and produce-packed, but with such a different soul. Here's where you pick up the ultimate half sours, bagels, Nova lox, babka, rugelach, and such. Shopping at Zabar's makes you think about how you'll get it all on the plate, not about what the plate will look like, as at D&D.

🏠 E2 ✉️ 2245 Broadway (80th St) ☎️ 212/787 2000 🚇 1, 9 79th St

Picnic spots

These don't start and end in Central Park. Some more to try:

Lower Manhattan: Battery Park City – benches and views all along the Hudson South Street Seaport boardwalk.

SoHo: The 'Vest Pocket Park' at Spring and Mulberry Streets, and the playground outside Coles Sports Center, Mercer and Houston Streets.

Greenwich Village: The ballpark at Clarkson and Hudson Streets, and St Luke's Garden at Hudson (Barrow/Grove Streets) – a well-kept secret, it's perfect! Union Square Park for the Greenmarket.

Midtown East: Greenacre Park at 51st Street and Second Avenue (what a misnomer). New York Public Library steps or tables at Bryant Park. Crystal Pavilion (Third Ave/50th St), and Paley Park (53rd St/Fifth Ave) concrete canyon with waterfall.

Midtown West: Equitable Tower Atrium on Seventh Ave, 51st–52nd streets – greenery!

Upper East Side: Carl Schurz Park, East End Ave, 84–89th streets. Gracie Mansion, where the mayor lives is here, also great Roosevelt Island and bridge views.

NOWHERE BUT NEW YORK

Summertime

You know it's summer when the block fairs descend. Every Sunday, at least one Manhattan block of blocks sprouts a forest of police hurdles, and the air thickens with the distinctive aroma of frying zeppole and bratwurst. At first, these collections of stalls are charm itself, but after a while, they begin to look samey: The same stalls with the same hand-painted batik leather-thonged jackets; the same troupe of Andean nose-flautists flogging copies of their CD; the same person eating the same falafel. This is no less true if you pass two on the same day, since they are able to clone at will. It would be a benign phenomenon if unscrupulous entrepreneurs didn't cream all the profits, but they do. There are better things to do on a Sunday.

GOOD GIFTS

CASWELL-MASSEY

If your hotel's a fancy one, chances are they stocked your bathroom with smellies from here.
✚ E6 ✉ 518 Lexington Ave
☎ 212/755 2254 🚇 6 51th St

ENCHANTED FOREST

Children have to be taken to this aptly-named grotto of stuffed animals and fairy-tale things.
✚ C10 ✉ 85 Mercer St
☎ 212/925 6677 🚇 N, R Prince St

FIREFIGHTER'S FRIEND

Yes, it's the NYFD's shop, selling the essential souvenirs: Keep Back 200-Ft T-shirts, and metal-clamp-fastened oilskins, long purloined by the fashion crowd.
✚ C10 ✉ 263 Lafayette St
☎ 212/226 3142 🚇 6 Spring

GUGGENHEIM MUSEUM STORE

From investment pieces to trinkets, and all in the best possible, most modern, taste.
✚ C10 ✉ 575 Broadway
☎ 212/423 3875 🚇 N, R Prince St

KATE'S PAPERIE

You think a paper shop would be dull? Try this, and weep. Many paper-related *objets* too.
✚ C10 ✉ 561 Broadway
☎ 212/941 9816 🚇 N, R Prince St

M.A.C.

Women (and drag queens) who wear any make up at all, ever, ought to know this cult range of pigment-rich cosmetics. It's the one that employs RuPaul as its 'Spokesmodel'.
✚ C9 ✉ 14 Christopher St
☎ 212/243 4150 🚇 A, B, C, D, E, F W4th St

PEARL PAINT

Five floors of rock-bottom priced art supplies, craft materials, stationery, frames, etc.
✚ B11 ✉ 308 Canal St
(Broadway) ☎ 212/431 7932
🚇 N, R Canal St

THE STRAND

More a way of life than a bookstore, or so you'll find when you get lost in its 'eight miles' of second-hand and remaindered books, and half-price review copies. They do searches.
✚ C9 ✉ 828 Broadway
☎ 212/473 1452 🚇 N, R, 4, 6 Union Sq

HOME

BROADWAY PANHANDLER

Not the most comprehensive of all kitchen supply stores, but one of the best priced, with wares good enough for the semi-pro.
✚ C10 ✉ 520 Broadway
(Spring St) ☎ 212/966 3434
🚇 N, R Prince St

PRATESI

Fabulous costly linens.
✚ F4 ✉ 829 Madison Ave
(69th St) ☎ 212/288 2315
🚇 6 68th St

SOHO MILL

Bargain linens, mostly seconds of major ranges. Especially good for towels.
✚ C10 ✉ 490 Broadway, 2nd Floor ☎ 212/226 8040 🚇 N, R Prince St

WOOLFMAN-GOLD & GOOD

This pioneer of all SoHo's million interiors stores is still the clear leader of trends in tabletops.
✚ C10 ✉ 116 Greene St ☎ 212/431 1888 🚇 N, R Prince St

STRANGE

ASTOR PLACE HAIRSTYLISTS

More of a theatre than a store. Many a famous head's been shorn here.
✚ C9 ✉ 2 Astor Place ☎ 212/475 9854 🚇 6 Astor Place

CHARLES' PLACE INC

Charles Elkaim forges flamboyant, fun jewellery out of miniatures and rhinestones. He also sells doll's house furniture and mint vintage toy cars.
✚ C10 ✉ 234 Mulberry St ☎ 212/966 7302 🚇 6 Spring

THE EROTIC BAKER

The name is no lie. Get a fudge-frosted phallus here. Special orders take 24 hours.
✚ E1 ✉ 582 Amsterdam Ave (88th St) ☎ 212/362 7557 🚇 1, 9 86th St

THE FAN CLUB

Do you feel the need to own Dolly Parton's blouse? Audrey Hepburn's slacks? Here they are, for real.
✚ C8 ✉ 22 W 19th St ☎ 212/929 3349 🚇 1, 2, 3 14th St

SILLY

LITTLE RICKIE'S

Everybody's favourite indulgence is this retirement home for the novelty items of five decades: glue-on beauty marks, ant farms, wind-up teeth, and excellent cards.
✚ D10 ✉ 491/2 First Ave (3rd St) ☎ 212/505 6467 🚇 F 2nd Ave

LOVE SAVES THE DAY

This – ostensibly a vintage clothes store – is crammed with mauve circus spangles, 1950s Barbies, Cliff Richard disguise kits, Elvis wigs – you get the picture. Rosanna Arquette bought Madonna's jacket here in *Desperately Seeking Susan*.
✚ D10 ✉ 119 Second Ave ☎ 212/228 3802 🚇 F 2nd Ave

WEIRD

MAXILLA & MANDIBLE

Bones are the basic merchandise here, with related butterflies, shells, and antlers.
✚ E2 ✉ 453 Columbus Ave (81st St) ☎ 212/724 6173 🚇 C 81st St

PANDORA'S BOX

It's hard to move for the plaster cherubs, Nefertitis, columns and wherever you look, an Elvis.
✚ B10 ✉ 153 Prince St ☎ 212/505 7615 🚇 C, E Spring St

PARACELSO

'I have exquisite taste' says Luxor, who has blue eyebrows and hails from Milan. Her store beams with cloth-of-gold, sequins, striped chiffons and velvets, like a magpie's nest.
✚ B10 ✉ 414 W Broadway ☎ 212/966 4232 🚇 C, E Spring St

Flea markets

In a city whose best junk shops are more interested in renting out pieces for movie set dressing than selling them, such markets flourish. The prime flea is the Annex (✉ Sixth Ave/26th St ☎ 212/243 5343 🕐 Sat, Sun), long-established, antique-y and huge with a small charge for admission. Second is the far newer, but similar, SoHo (✉ Broadway/Grand St ☎ 212/682 2000 🕐 Sat, Sun). The Annex has an adjunct, the Garage (✉ 112 W 25th St ☎ 212/647 0707 🕐 Sat, Sun), which isn't a real flea because it's indoors. Two uptown include crafts and greenmarket stalls with the antiques and bric-à-brac: the I.S. 44 Green Flea (✉ Columbus Ave/ 77th St ☎ 212/721 0900 🕐 Sun), and the inside-outside P.S. 183 (✉ E 67th St/ York Ave 🕐 Sat).

BARS & COFFEE BARS

Cocktails

Although, on the whole, New Yorkers aren't great drinkers, there's a renewed interest in cocktails – think very dry martinis with an olive rather than scarlet alcoholic slushpuppies. But where to order one?

Lounge bars:

Fez

✉ 380 Lafayette St

☎ 212/533 2680

Match

✉ 160 Mercer St (Houston St)

☎ 212/343 0020

Merc Bar

✉ 151 Mercer St

☎ 212/966 2727

Temple Bar

✉ 332 Lafayette St

☎ 212/925 4242

Skyline gazing:

Top of the Sixes

✉ 666 Fifth Ave

☎ 212/757 6662

Rainbow Room (►68)

Top of the Tower

✉ Beekman 3 Mitchell Place

☎ 212/355 7300

Old Manhattan: '21' Club (►65)

The Jockey Club

✉ 112 Central Park S

☎ 212/757 9494

King Cole Bar

✉ St Regis Hotel, 2 E55th St

☎ 212/753 4500

CAFFEINE

CAFFÈ REGGIO

The original, pre-coffee bar craze, Roman rococo, bohemian espresso house.

✚ B10 ✉ 119 MacDougal St

☎ 212/475 9557 🚇 A, B, C, D, E, F W4th St

EUREKA JOE

This is no Starbucks (the Seattle chain), this is a lovely, light lounge with couches and cake.

✚ C8 ✉ 168 Fifth Ave

☎ 212/741 7500 🚇 L, N, R Union Sq

JONATHAN MORR ESPRESSO BAR

Midtown's fanciest aluminum bean palace. Dig those cup sconces.

✚ E5 ✉ 1394 Sixth Ave (57th St) ☎ 212/757 6677 🚇 B, Q 57th St

HOTELS

OAK BAR

Classic city swank at the Plaza.

✚ E5 ✉ Fifth Ave (59th St)

☎ 212/759 3000 🚇 N, R 5th Ave

PEN TOP LOUNGE

Way up high, and glazed all round like a sputnik spacecraft on the roof. What views!

✚ E5 ✉ Peninsula, 700 Fifth Ave (54th St) ☎ 212/247 2200 🚇 N, R 5th Ave

VODKA BAR

Teeny and *haute* style – feels like being trapped in a Bridget Riley canvas.

✚ D6 ✉ Royalton, 44 W44th St ☎ 212/944 8844 🚇 B, D, F, 42nd St

LITERARY BEER

LION'S HEAD

See the wall of book jackets – many regulars stagger home and actually write. A Village classic.

✚ B9 ✉ 59 Christopher St

☎ 212/929 0670 🚇 1, 9 Christopher St

PETE'S TAVERN

The 1864 Gramercy Park Victorian where O Henry wrote *The Gift of the Magi*.

✚ D9 ✉ 129 E18th St

☎ 212/473 7676 🚇 N, R, 4, 6 Union Sq

WHITE HORSE TAVERN

Here Dylan Thomas drank his last. A picturesque Village pub.

✚ B9 ✉ 567 Hudson St

☎ 212/243 9260 🚇 1, 9 Christopher St

BEER

D.B.A.

An East Village dive that takes beer more seriously than itself. What's it mean? 'doing business as'.

✚ D10 ✉ 41 First Ave

☎ 212/475 5097

🚇 F 2nd Ave

MCSORLEY'S OLD ALE HOUSE

Someone will show you this sawdust-floor tavern and tell you it's historic (1854).

✚ D10 ✉ 15 E7th St

☎ 212/473 9148 🚇 6 Astor Place

ZIP CITY BREWING CO

The first of the growing number of Manhattan microbreweries.

✚ C8 ✉ 3 W18th St (Fifth Ave) ☎ 212/366 6333

🚇 F 14th St

PERFORMANCE

BROADWAY

The word is the quint-essence of glamour and sparkle, but the district is lousy with porn palaces and clip joints. There *is* a Times Square redevelop-ment plan, with artists roped in to bedeck dark awnings with creative pro-jects and building works in progress, but gaudiness and a faint scent of danger is really part of the seedy neon charm. Broadway is the area between 42nd and 53rd streets, and Sixth to Ninth avenues.

OFF AND OFF-OFF

BAM
Or Brooklyn Academy of Music, which mounts major cutting-edge work in every discipline.
Off I14 ⊠ 30 Lafayette Ave, Brooklyn ☎ 718/636 4100 ⓐ A, C Lafayette Ave

THE FANTASTICKS
Not the name of the theatre, but of the loved musical that's been running since 1960.
B9 ⊠ Sullivan, 181 Sullivan St ☎ 212/674 3838 ⓐ 1, 9 Christopher St

JOSEPH PAPP PUBLIC THEATER
This has two stages and is named after its visionary and tireless founder.
C10 ⊠ 425 Lafayette St ☎ 212/598 7150 ⓐ B, D, F Broadway Lafayette St

LA MAMA E.T.C.
The pace-setter down-town, having debuted many a triumph.
D10 ⊠ 74A E4 St ☎ 212/ 475 7710 ⓐ F 2nd Ave

MITZI E. NEWHOUSE & VIVIAN BEAUMONT
The Lincoln Center's two theatres both stage established playwrights' work, often with famous actors. The latter is bigger.
D4 ⊠ Lincoln Center ☎ 212/362 7600 ⓐ 1, 9 66th St

PERFORMANCE GARAGE
This is where the avant-garde Wooster Group mount their challenging multimedia performances.
B10 ⊠ 33 Wooster St ☎ 212/966 3651 ⓐ C, E Spring St

THE OPERA

AMATO OPERA
A hollowed-out East Village brownstone, mounting full-length grand opera in miniature.
D10 ⊠ 319 Bowery ☎ 212/228 8200 ⓐ F 2nd Ave

THE METROPOLITAN OPERA
On a first night this is *so* glamorous. Never mind the singers – the Franco Zefirelli productions are the visual equivalent of Belgian cream truffles. Seasons: Oct–Apr.
D4 ⊠ Lincoln Center ☎ 212/362 6000 ⓐ 1, 9 66th St

NEW YORK CITY OPERA
Occupies the nextdoor auditorium Sept–Nov and Mar–Apr. Offers newer works, operetta, and the odd musical alongside the grands.
D4 ⊠ Lincoln Center ☎ 212/870 5570 ⓐ 1, 9 66th St

Where to get information

The *Village Voice's* shrinking readership suggests it's lost its touch, though it's still famous – for the least user-friendly listings.

The *New York Times* may not contain deathless prose, but listings in its Friday Weekend section are good, and the Sunday reviews are readable.

New York Magazine raised itself from the dead when scurrilous *Spy's* ex-editor took over. The most colourful and gossipy of the lot, and easy to use.

The *New Yorker* is far, far more than mere listings, of course. Its Goings on About Town has sections on every cultural corner (even restaurants).

New York Press is the cheapest way to get information – pick up this determinedly downtown paper for free at stores, movie theatres, etc.

ON THE TOWN

Lesbian and Gay Pride Week

The week in late June around the Stonewall anniversary is Lesbian and Gay Pride Week, which no longer resembles a 1970s-style angry activists' march, but is an excuse for highly visible partying. The terrible toll of AIDS has not dented the spirits of the community it hit the hardest, but rather has reconfirmed it. For proof, attend another of the city's favourite events – the annual, celebrity-studded AIDS Danceathon.
To help differentiate between the thousands of clubs, bars, restaurants, and so on, drop in for a chat at the Lesbian and Gay Community Center (✉ 208 W13th St ☎ 212/620 7310), or call the Switchboard (☎ 212/777 1800).

SHOWTIME

CAFÉ CARLYLE
The Upper East Side's absolutely elegant, pastel-coloured *boîte*.
✚ F4 ✉ Carlyle Hotel, Madison Ave (76th St) ☎ 212/744 1600 🚇 6 68th St

THE DUPLEX
Cabaret minus attitude – less need to dress at this Village version of a torch singer's showcase.
✚ B9 ✉ 61 Christopher St ☎ 212/255 5438 🚇 1, 9 Christopher St

KAPTAIN BANANA
A much more civilised way to absorb an over-the-top transvestite musical extravaganza than Wigstock, though the French dinner isn't gonna win any stars. Must book.
✚ C10 ✉ 101 Greene St ☎ 212/343 9000 🚇 N, R Prince St

TATOU
There's carnival (Wed–Sat) on Tatou's ornate crimson and gilt-framed stage; a dance floor and jazz all week – and a talented chef.
✚ F6 ✉ 151 E50th St ☎ 212/753 1144 🚇 6 51st St

COMEDY

BLUE MAN GROUP
Over five years of this trio's exceedingly mucky (paint-, not porn-spattered) *Tubes*, and everyone's still rolling in the aisles, kids included.
✚ C10 ✉ Astor Place Theatre, 434 Lafayette St ☎ 212/254 4370 🚇 B, D, F Broadway Lafayette St

CAROLINE'S COMEDY CLUB
More of the already-made-it than the up-and-coming play here, in theatreland.
✚ D5 ✉ 1626 Broadway (49th St) ☎ 212/757 4100 🚇 1, 9 50th St

JAZZ

BLUE NOTE
You'll fork out a lot to catch a big name at this famed Village club. They all come to NYC, and most stop off here and/or at the Vanguard.
✚ C9 ✉ 131 W3rd St ☎ 212/475 8592 🚇 A, B, C, D, E, F W4th St

BRADLEY'S
Small, wood-panelled, neighbourhoody, there's a dinner hour pianist, but it's best very late.
✚ C9 ✉ 70 University Place (11th St) ☎ 212/228 6440 🚇 6 Astor Place

IRIDIUM
By Lincoln Center is this upstart with cartoon decor. Try Mingus Mondays.
✚ D4 ✉ 44 W63rd St ☎ 212/582 2121 🚇 1, 9 66th St

KNITTING FACTORY
Moderns play this relocated factory of cool; but also beboppers and funksters.
✚ B11 ✉ 74 Leonard St (Broadway) ☎ 212/219 3055 🚇 1, 9 Franklin St

VILLAGE VANGUARD
This basement is the *ne plus ultra* of the jazz dive, 60 years old in 1995, and thriving. If you take in only one gig, make it here.
✚ B9 ✉ 178 Seventh Ave S

(11th St) ☎ 212/255 4037
🚇 1, 9 Christopher St

CLUBBING

NELL'S
Nell Campbell's two-level lounge/naughty dancing club endures, attracting all ages and types.
➕ B8 ✉ 246 W14th St
☎ 212/675 1567 🚇 A, C, E 14th St

REBAR
A long, narrow, friendly Chelsea club, with penchant for Britishness, and much enthusiasm on the dance floor.
➕ B8 ✉ 127 W16th St
☎ 212/627 1680 🚇 A, C, E 14th St

S.O.B.'S
The absolute number one for the Latin beat is the tropically decorated 'Sounds Of Brazil' – also for African sounds, reggae and other island music.
➕ B10 ✉ 204 Varick St
☎ 212/243 4940 🚇 1, 9 Canal St

TUNNEL
Hard and hip.
➕ B7 ✉ 47 W20th St
☎ 212/695 7292 🚇 C, E 23rd St

WEBSTER HALL
The very big East Village place that used to be the coolest.
➕ D9 ✉ 125 E11th St
☎ 212/353 1600 🚇 6 Astor Place

MUSIC FOR YOUTH

BROWNIE'S
Nose to tail in Alphabet City, slackers catch the local heroes. If the band *du jour* isn't here, look into No Tell Motel, next door.
➕ D10 ✉ 160 Ave A (11th St)
☎ 212/420 8392
🚇 F 2nd Ave

CBGB & OMFUG
Still alive long after giving birth to Yank punk rock, this teenage steam room has spread all over the block, with a sweet 'unplugged' café next door. (It's 'Country, Blue Grass, Blues, & Other Music For Uplifting Gourmandizers'.)
➕ C10 ✉ 315 Bowery
☎ 212/982 4052
🚇 F 2nd Ave

MERCURY LOUNGE
A laid-back atmosphere attracts the most listened-to performers at their zenith of hotness.
➕ D11 ✉ 217 E Houston St
☎ 212/260 4700 🚇 F 2nd Ave

MUSIC FOR ALL

IRVING PLAZA
Medium-big people, ranging from They Might Be Giants to Paul Simon, play this galleried Gramercy hall.
➕ D9 ✉ 17 Irving Place
☎ 212/777 6800 🚇 N, R, 4, 6 Union Sq

MADISON SQUARE GARDEN
Hosts the rock giants (➤ 17).

TRAMPS
A hall that gives great atmosphere for rootsy bluesy bands (the Meters are regulars) and indie rock.
➕ C8 ✉ 45 W21st St
☎ 212/727 7788 🚇 F 23rd St

Gay New York

The subject merits several books of its own. This is one of the best cities in which to be gay, with a thriving, pulsating community for both genders, and all in betweens. The city shares the honours with San Francisco for launching 'gay lib' in the US, with Stonewall (➤ 31) playing a major role, and it still leads the world in everything from AIDS activism to spawning gorgeous transvestites. Yes, if the Lady Bunny, Lipsynka and, of course, RuPaul mean anything to you, this city is going to feel very comfortable. All three girls are New Yorkers, and – if their busy schedules allow – all make large appearances at that annual celebration of vogueing and dishing, Wigstock (➤ 60).

81

Free Summer Entertainment

August in Manhattan

August is a wicked month in Manhattan, with temperatures that regularly make it to three figures, and – even worse – humidity that frizzes hair and soaks T-shirts as soon as you step outside. The street noise level rises too, and so do tempers. It's no wonder New Yorkers desert the city every weekend. An entire culture revolves around summer rentals and summer shares, and whether you're a houseguest in the right place and whether your houseguests are the right houseguests, but this will probably pass most visitors by entirely. And so it should, because what really matters is how, every weekend for a whole month, the city belongs to you. Theatres and movie theatres are half empty; Central Park lacks its usual rollerblade traffic jams; it takes less than an hour to cross town in a cab and, best of all, you can get a table almost anywhere without reservations.

MUSIC

CENTRAL PARK SUMMER STAGE

This is a great free festival of such variety that the person does not exist who doesn't want to see at least three events. Sponsors' concession stands ring the stage, and many people bring picnics.

✚ F4 ⊠ Naumberg Bandshell (72nd St) ☎ 212/ 360 2777 🚇 Jun–Aug 🚇 C 72nd St

LINCOLN CENTER OUT-OF-DOORS

By no means just music, this is an admirable summerlong fiesta of 100-odd varied events.

✚ D4 ⊠ 62nd–66th streets ☎ 212/872 5400 🚇 1, 9 66th St

THE NEW YORK PHILHARMONIC

They don't only come out on 4 July, but do a whole season of free park concerts ☎ 212/875 5030 🚇 Jul–Aug

METROPOLITAN OPERA IN THE PARKS

As above.
☎ 212/362 6000

WORLD FINANCIAL CENTER

The Plaza has lots of free concerts, all season.

THEATRE

SHAKESPEARE IN THE PARK

This much-loved festival is mounted by the Public Theater and consists of two Bard works per season. Though tickets are gratis, you must queue in the morning and can take only two.

✚ F2 ⊠ Delacorte Theater, Central Park ☎ 212/598 7100 🚇 Jul–Aug 🚇 B, C 81st St

DANCING

MIDSUMMER NIGHT SWING

'Dances under the Stars' is the subtitle for this weekly public party.

✚ D4 ⊠ Lincoln Center Plaza ☎ 212/875 5400 🚇 Jun–Jul 🚇 1, 9 66th St

FESTIVALS

NINTH AVENUE INTERNATIONAL FOOD FESTIVAL

Culinary nirvana.

✚ D4/D5/C6 ⊠ Ninth Ave (37–57th St) ☎ 212/581 7217 🚇 10AM–7PM, 3rd weekend May 🚇 C, E 50th St

MUSEUM MILE FESTIVAL

Crowds perambulate Fifth Avenue, visiting museums for free.

✚ G1–3 ⊠ Fifth Ave (82–102nd streets) 🚇 6–9PM, Jun 🚇 4, 5, 6 86th St

THE FOURTH OF JULY

Celebrations kick off at the Stars and Stripes Regatta (⊠ South Street Seaport ☎ 212/669 9400 🚇 3–4 Jul), with accompanying concerts on the pier. At night, there are two things to do. The New York Philharmonic plays a concert in Central Park, with a firework finale (☎ 212/875 5030), and Macy's shoots millions of dollars into the sky over the Lower Hudson in a full half hour of pyrotechnics (☎ 212/ 494 5432). Good vantage points get very crammed. Consider Brooklyn.

THIS SPORTING TOWN

WATCHING

KNICKERBOCKERS
Basketball may now have more New York fans than baseball, football and hockey, thanks to this heart-breaking team, who keep getting close – but no cigar. If you manage to get tickets you'll certainly see celebs courtside – Madonna and Woody Allen are diehard Knicks fans.
✚ C7 ✉ Madison Square Garden ☎ 212/465 6741 🕙 Oct–Apr 🚇 1, 2, 3 34th St

NEW YORK RANGERS
The hockey team is also worshipped – for winning the 1994 Stanley Cup, and also for Mark Messier. Hockey season runs Oct–Apr.
✚ C7 ✉ Madison Square Garden ☎ 212/465 6741 🕙 Oct–Apr 🚇 1, 2, 3 34th St

The Islanders and the New Jersey Devils have a smattering of NY fans too.
(✉ Nassau Coliseum, Long Island ☎ 516/888 9000) (✉ Meadowlands ☎ 201/935 3900)

THE GIANTS AND THE JETS
The former have more fans than the latter, though both teams play in the same stadium. You don't have much hope of seeing either of them, since nearly all tickets sold are sold as season tickets.
✉ Giants Stadium, East Rutherford, NJ ☎ (Giants) 201/935 8222; (Jets) 516/538 6600 🕙 Sep–Dec

THE YANKEES AND THE METS
They play in different leagues and are very different propositions, the more so the more you know about baseball. But even if you know squat, the Mets Shea Stadium is soulless compared to Yankee Stadium.
✉ Shea Stadium, Flushing, Queens ☎ 718/507 8499; Yankee Stadium, ➤ 47 🕙 Apr–Oct

DOING
(Also ➤ 59)

CYCLING
Join the Central Park pack. Rent clunky bikes from: ✉ Loeb Boathouse, Central Park, near E74 St ☎ 212/861 4137. Good machines from: ✉ Metro Bikes, 1311 Lexington Ave (88th St) ☎ 212/427 4450

IN-LINE SKATING
Learn to brake at the Wollman Rink (✉ Fifth Ave (59th St) ☎ 212/517 4800), then rent – or buy – from Peck & Goodie (✉ 919 Eighth Ave (54th St) ☎ 212/246 6123)

ROCK CLIMBING
If you already can, then bring your shoes for Central Park bouldering – or the wall at Manhattan Plaza Health Club if you're desperate (✉ 450 W43rd St ☎ 212/594 0554). If you want to learn, the NYC Outward Bound Center runs beginner and intermediate classes (☎ 212/348 4867).

RUNNING
By far the most-run place in the city is the 1.58 mile Central Park Reservoir track. The New York Road Runners Club has an all-season schedule and welcomes visitors (☎ 212/860 4455).

Party runners

A festive New York tradition, most suited to a city where the gym is frequently the second home, is the New Year's Eve Central Park Runner's World Midnight Run. Beginning with a costume ball, culminating in fireworks, and with a five-mile race in the middle, this none-too-serious athletic event attracts thousands of weekend (or year-end) warriors, many dressed to party. The start line is Tavern on the Green, and advance registration is around $5 (☎ 212/860 4455), which includes admission to the ball. Not all entrants get around to running, say the organisers.

83

LUXURY HOTELS

The hotels on the following pages are in three categories. Expect to pay per night for a double room
Luxury Hotels: over $140
Mid-Range Hotels: $80–$140
Budget Accommodation: under $80

Will it, won't it, will it, won't it ...

Will the Mercer be the first hotel in sleek SoHo, or will the upstart SoHo Grand have beaten it to the post by the time you read this? Most of the work on The Mercer Hotel, opposite the Guggenheim, was already complete, when it ran into engineering and legal problems and had to stall its already much-publicised opening. Meanwhile, plans were proceeding apace for a new building to go in an empty lot on West Broadway near Grand Street. The SoHo Grand should fill another gap too – the one for affordable hotel rooms downtown.

84

CARLYLE
Visiting minor European royalty holes up in this 38-storey patrician palace on the Upper East Side, and trust funders keep an apartment for when they're not wintering in Gstaad. It's *fin de siècle* perfection to behold.
➕ F4 ✉ 35 E76th St
☎ 212/744 1600 🍴 Carlyle Restaurant, the Gallery, Café Carlyle, Bemelmans Bar 🚇 6 68th St

FOUR SEASONS
This newest New York grand has two things in common with its namesake restaurant: absolute glamour and a household-name architect (I M Pei of the Paris Louvre pyramids). It's spacious to the point of inducing agoraphobia.
➕ E5 ✉ 57 E57th St
☎ 212/758 5700 🍴 5757 🚇 B, Q 57th St

THE MARK
This exquisite and peaceful townhouse-mansion a couple of blocks from the park on the Upper East Side, features antiques and calm, goose-down pillows, palms, Piranesi prints, and (mostly) your own kitchen.
➕ F3 ✉ 25 E77th St
☎ 212/744 4300 🍴 Mark's 🚇 6 77th St

MAYFAIR
The house of Le Cirque has long been revered as the top dog for its size (medium), but had a little financial trouble at press time. Perhaps the high-maintainance service (orchids in the bathroom, choice of toiletries, a library of pillows, from

full-body to anti-snore) that accompanies the Jamesian, Wharton-esque moneyed décor was too good to bear.
➕ F4 ✉ 610 Park Ave
☎ 212/288 0800
🍴 Le Cirque 🚇 6 68th St

PLAZA
Oh what can you say about this star of screen (*Plaza Suite*, etc), and page (Eloise, who lived here) and gossip column (Trump, who bought it and married Marla in it). The rooms aren't the best in town, but its profile is, and so is the location (corner of Fifth, across from the park).
➕ E5 ✉ 768 Fifth Ave
☎ 212/759 3000 🍴 Palm Court, Oak Room, Edwardian Room, Gauguin 🚇 N, R 5th Ave

PLAZA ATHENÉE
Parisian splendour on the Upper East Side, this manageably sized (160-room) Forte French copy is known for its amazing duplex penthouses, its security (Princess Di was here) and *comme il faut* service.
➕ F4 ✉ 37 E64th St
☎ 212/734 9100
🍴 Le Régence 🚇 N, R 5th Ave

RITZ-CARLTON
Back on track after many renovations, the English-style (meaning wood panelling) R–C, at the other end of Central Park South from Essex House, shares those park views, for which you pay more. The elegantissimo Italian restaurant panders to wealthier guests.
➕ E5 ✉ 112 Central Park South ☎ 212/757 1900
🍴 Fantino 🚇 B, Q 57th St

MID-RANGE HOTELS

HOTEL BEACON
This Lincoln Center/
Central Park neighbour
looks and feels far more
expensive than it is. It has
very spacious rooms with
kitchenettes, cable TV,
big closets, and your own
voice mail on the phone.
⊞ E2 ✉ 2130 Broadway
(75th St) ☎ 212/787 1100
🚇 1, 2, 3 72nd St

FITZPATRICK
The sole US representa-
tive of the family-owned
Dublin chain, this place
on the easterly side of
midtown has the charm of
the Irish in abundance. It
stands out for service,
good taste – and the
perfect brunch.
⊞ F5 ✉ 687 Lexington Ave
☎ 212/355 0100 🍴 Fitzers
🚇 4, 6 59th St

FRANKLIN
The first of Bernard
Goldberg's remarkable,
small but growing, collection of elegant boutique
hotels that look like
luxury but at a chain store
price. Any sacrifice is in
room size, not high-style
details like cedar-lined
closets ...
⊞ G3 ✉ 164 E87th St
☎ 212/369 1000 🚇 4, 5, 6
86th St

GRAMERCY PARK
Popular with visiting BBC
people and other Britons,
this charmer offers the
keys to the private,
eponymous park, small,
quiet, shabby rooms, and a
perfect Cole Porter-esque
piano bar. Has its own art
festival too.
⊞ D8 ✉ 2 Lexington Ave
☎ 212/475 4320
🍴 Restaurant 🚇 6 23rd St

MAYFLOWER
Hard to find fault with this
classic. The décor's been
recently refreshed, the
location – by Lincoln
Center/Columbus Circle –
is perfect for pleasure,
business, and running (get
a park view room and
you'll never leave); service
is nurturing. It's lovable.
⊞ E4 ✉ Central Park West at
61st St ☎ 212/265 0060
🍴 The Conservatory 🚇 A, C, D
1 59th St

MORGAN
Ian Schrager and the late
Steve Rubell created the
1980s in the ultimate disco,
Studio 54; they also
created this, the first of
three design-conscious
hotels (the Royalton is
number two, and see the
Paramount, page 86). The
Andrée Putnam-designed
monochrome suites have
Mapplethorpe prints and
are among the most private
in NYC – there's no sign.
⊞ D7 ✉ 237 Madison Ave
☎ 212/686 0300 🚇 6 33rd St

SHOREHAM
The Franklin's younger
midtown sister is a beauty.
Grey, black and metallic
décor, with cedar closets,
CD players and VCRs in
every room.
⊞ E5 ✉ 33 W55th St
☎ 212/247 6700 🚇 E, F
5th Ave

WASHINGTON
SQUARE
The Village's only hotel
recently injected a lot of
cash, so is very comfort-
able, despite the lack of
bellhops and such..
⊞ C9 ✉ 103 Waverley Place
☎ 212/777 9515 🍴 CIII
🚇 1, 9 Christopher St

The Algonquin

The Algonquin is forever
associated with the only group of
literary wits to be named after a
piece of furniture: the Algonquin
Round Table. Not quite the
Bloomsbury Group, the *bon
viveurs* achieved almost as much
at the bar here as they did in the
pages of the embryo *New
Yorker*, with Robert Benchley,
Dorothy Parker and Alexander
Woolcott particularly well
ensconced. The hotel's Rose
Room still contains the very
table, and the *New Yorker's*
offices still decant straight into
the hotel.

85

BUDGET ACCOMMODATION

B&Bs

Those who prefer real neighbourhoods, authentic experiences and behaving like a local, may opt for a B&B. Often these are found in Brooklyn brownstones, where the host has an extra room. Others are empty apartments. The only imperative is to book ahead. Try:

Abode Bed and Breakfasts Ltd
- ✉ Box 20022, 10028
- ☎ 212/472 2000

Bed and Breakfast Network of New York
- ✉ 134 W32nd St, Suite 602, 10001
- ☎ 212/645 8134

Inn New York
- ✉ 266 W71st St 10023
- ☎ 212/580 1900

New World Bed and Breakfast
- ✉ 150 Fifth Ave, Suite 711, 10011
- ☎ 212/675 5600

Urban Ventures
- ✉ Box 426, 10024
- ☎ 212/594 5650

CARLTON ARMS

The wackiest hotel in New York has every surface covered in lurid murals done by artist guests. The comfort level's basic, but it's friendly. As it says on the business card: 'This ain't no Holiday Inn'.
- ✚ D8 ✉ 160 E25th St
- ☎ 212/684 8337 🚇 6 23rd St

EXCELSIOR

Overlooking the Natural History Museum, this is reminiscent of a faded boulevard hotel in Paris, perhaps in the 1950s. All the big, clean, fluorescent-lit rooms have kitchenettes and a great deal of blue in the décor.
- ✚ E2 ✉ 45 W81st St
- ☎ 212/362 9200 🍴 Coffee shop 🚇 B, C 81st St

GERSCHWIN

'We're just at the edge of hip,' says the manager of this first New York Interclub hotel – Urs Jakob's decidedly arts-orientated string of superhostels. Art elevates the style of basic rooms, and bars, roofdecks and lounges encourage sociability.
- ✚ D8 ✉ 7 E27th St
- ☎ 212/545 8000 🍴 Café 🚇 N, R 23rd St

MILBURN

This is such a friendly place that you become immune to the mismatched furniture in the bargain suites. These have shabby corners, but tons of space and facilities, including kitchens.
- ✚ E2 ✉ 242 W76th St
- ☎ 212/362 5476 🚇 1, 2, 3 72nd St

OFF SOHO SUITES

It's ten blocks to SoHo (ditto the East Village) from here, which makes the location officially bad. This translates into spacious suites with marble bathroom, full kitchen, phone, TV, a/c, in an area which young and arty people often prefer. Décor is plasticy.
- ✚ C11 ✉ 11 Rivington St
- ☎ 212/979 9808 🍴 Le Gourmet Deli, SoHo Suites Café
- 🚇 F 2nd Ave

PARAMOUNT

The best deal in the city for the visually sensitive, this bears the stunning stamp of Philippe Starck, even in the famously tiny rooms. All fashionable budget-watchers stay here.
- ✚ D5 ✉ 235 W46 St
- ☎ 212/764 5500
- 🍴 Restaurant, Dean & Delucca
- 🚇 C, E 50th St

PARK SAVOY

The diametric opposite to the Paramount, the tiny rooms here are hideous to look at, a designer's never been near the place, and there's a (very helpful) front desk staff of one. However, it's one block back from Central Park South, with rock-bottom rates.
- ✚ E5 ✉ 158 W58th St
- ☎ 212/245 5755 🚇 B, Q 57th St

SEAPORT INN

A fairly new conversion a block or two from the water has unobjectionable chain hotel décor – it's a Best Western. The charm lies wholly in its situation.
- ✚ B12 ✉ 33 Peck Slip
- ☎ 212/766 6600 🚇 2, 3, 4 Fulton St

NEW YORK
travel facts

ARRIVING & DEPARTING

Before you go

- All visitors to the United States must have a valid full passport and a return ticket. For countries participating in the Visa Waiver Program, a visa is not required, though you must fill out the green visa-waiver form issued on the plane. You are also required to fill out a customs form (see below) and an immigration form.

When to go

- The New York winter can be severe, with heavy snow, biting winds and sub-freezing temperatures from December through February. It can be an ordeal to get around.
- Spring is unpredictable – even in April, snow showers can alternate with 'shirtsleeves' temperatures' – but the worst of winter is over by mid-March.
- Outdoor events start in earnest in May.
- July and August are extremely hot and humid (with occasional heavy rain), driving many New Yorkers out of town. However, during this time queues are shorter, restaurant reservations optional, outdoor festivals at their peak, and the city seems rather exotic. Air conditioning is universal, which helps.
- Autumn (fall) is generally thought the best time to visit. Warm temperatures persist into October (even November), with humidity dropping off in September.

Climate

- Average temperatures:
  Dec–Feb -2–6 C (29–43°F)
  Mar 1–8°C (34–47°F)
  Apr 7–16°C (45–61°F)
  May 12–21°C (54–70°F)

Jun 17–27°C (63–81°F)
Jul–Aug 20-32°C (68–90°F)
Sep 16–24°C (61–76°F)
Oct 11–19°C (52–67°F)
Nov 6–13°C (43–56°F).

Arriving by air

- Most international flights arrive at John F Kennedy (JFK) Airport in Queens, about 15 miles east of Manhattan. Fewer arrive at Newark, New Jersey, 16 miles west. Domestic flights arrive at La Guardia, Queens, 8 miles east.

JFK

- Taxi: $25–40, plus tolls and tip. Take only a licensed cab from the official ranks.
- Bus: Carey Airport Express Coach (☎718/632 0500), to six stops in Manhattan about every 30 minutes; Gray Line Air Shuttle (☎212/757 6840) shared minibus to any location.
- Helicopter: National Helicopter (☎800-645 3494), 10-minute trip to 34th St East Heliport.

Newark

- Taxi: $30–45, plus tolls and tip.
- Bus: Carey Airport Express, see above, NJ Transit Airport Express 300 (☎201/762 5100), to the Port Authority every 15 minutes; Olympia Trails Airport Express (☎212/964 6233) to Penn Station, Grand Central and WTC every 20 minutes. Gray Line as above.

Arriving by sea

- The QE2 still sails into the Passenger Ship Terminal (✉ Twelfth Ave (50–52nd St)).

Arriving by train

- Commuter trains (Metro-North) use Grand Central Terminal

(✉ 42nd St/Park Ave; ☎ 212/532 4900). Long-distance trains (AMTRAK) arrive at Pennsylvania Railroad Station (✉ 31st St Eighth Ave; ☎ 212/582 6875). PATH trains from the suburbs stop at several stations in Manhattan.

Arriving by bus
- Long distance (Greyhound) and commuter buses arrive at the Port Authority Terminal (✉ 42nd St Eighth Ave; ☎ 212/564 8484)

Customs regulations
- Non-US citizens may import duty-free: 1 quart (32 fl. oz.) alcohol, 200 cigarettes or 50 cigars, and up to $100-worth of gifts.
- Among restricted items for import are: meat, fruit, plants, seeds, lottery tickets.

ESSENTIAL FACTS

Travel Insurance
- It is essential to have adequate insurance coverage when travelling in the US, mainly because of the astronomical cost of medical procedures.
- A minimum of $1 million medical coverage is recommended for the US.
- Favour a policy which also includes trip cancellation, baggage and document loss.

Opening hours
- Banks: Mon–Fri 9–3 or 3:30; some open longer, and on Sat.
- Shops: Mon–Sat 10–6; many are open far later, and on Sun; those in the Village and SoHo open and close later.
- Museums: hours vary, but Mon is the most common closing day.
- Post offices: Mon–Fri 10–5 or 6.

- Of course, in the city that never sleeps, you'll find much open round the clock.

National holidays
- 1 January; third Monday in January (Martin Luther King Day); third Monday in February (Presidents' Day); Good Friday (half day); Easter Monday; last Monday in May (Memorial Day); 4 July (Independence Day); first Monday in September (Labor Day); second Monday in October (Columbus Day); 11 November (Veterans' Day); fourth Thursday in November (Thanksgiving Day); 25 December.

Money matters
- The unit of currency is the dollar (= 100 cents). Notes (bills) come in denominations of $1, $5, $10, $20, $50 and $100; coins are 25¢ (a quarter), 10¢ (a dime), 5¢ (a nickel) and 1¢ (a penny, increasingly optional).
- Nearly all banks have Automatic Teller Machines (ATMs), which accept cards registered in other countries that are linked to the Cirrus or Plus networks. Before leaving home, check which network your cards are linked to, and ensure your personal identification number is valid in the US, where six-figure numbers are the norm.
- Credit cards are also a widely accepted and secure alternative to cash.
- US dollar traveller's cheques function like cash in all but small shops; $20 and $50 denominations are the most useful. Don't bother trying to exchange these (or foreign currency) at the bank – it is more trouble than it's worth, and commissions are high.

Etiquette

- Tipping: waitstaff get 15–20% (roughly double the 8.25% sales tax at the bottom of the bill); so do taxi drivers. Bartenders get about the same (though less than $1 is mean), and will probably 'buy' you a drink if you're there a while. Bellhops ($1 per bag), room service waiters (10%), and hairdressers (15–20%) should also be tipped.

- Panhandlers: you will need to evolve a strategy for distributing change to the panhandlers among New York's immense homeless population. Some New Yorkers give once a day; some carry pockets of pennies; some give food; others give nothing on the street, but contribute a sum to a homelessness charity.

- Smoking: No longer a matter of politeness, there are ever more stringent smoking laws in New York. Smoking is banned on all public transport, in taxis, offices, shops, and – since April 1995 – in restaurants seating more than 35.

Safety

- As in any big city, maintain an awareness of your surroundings and of other people, and try to look as if you know your way around.

- Do not get involved with street crazies, however entertaining they may seem.

- The subway is probably best avoided at night, and also the Lower East Side, Alphabet City east of Avenue C, the far west of Midtown, and of Greenwich Village, and north of about 90th Street.

- Central Park is a no-go area after dark (except for performances), and the Financial District is eerily deserted – it's generally best to avoid deserted places at night.

- Apart from this, common-sense rules apply – conceal your wallet; keep the zip or clasp of your bag on the inside; do not flash large amounts of cash, gold and diamonds, etc.

Women travellers

- New York women are street-wise and outspoken, so if someone's bugging you, don't hold back on the insults – they'll be expecting it.

- Though less sleazy than in the past, the Times Square area is still miserable for women walking alone.

Places of worship

- Baptist: Memorial Baptist Church (✉ 141 W115th St; ☎ 212/663 8830). Tourists are welcomed (for a moderate charge) Sundays 10.45AM.

- Episcopal: Cathedral of St John the Divine (✉ 112th St/ Amsterdam Ave; ☎ 212/316 7400), services at 8, 9, 11AM, 7PM; Grace Church (✉ 802 Broadway/10th St; ☎ 212/254 2000) services at 9, 11 AM.

- Jewish: Temple Emanu-El (✉ 1 E65th St; ☎ 212/744 1400) services at 5:30PM.

- Methodist: Christ Church United Methodist (✉ Park Ave/ 60th St; ☎ 212/838 3036) services 9, 11AM.

- Roman Catholic: St Patrick's Cathedral (✉ Fifth Ave/50th St; ☎ 212/753 2261).

Students

- An International Student Identity Card (ISIC) is good for reduced admission at museums, theatres, tours and other attractions.

- Carry the ISIC or other photo ID at all times, to prove you're over

21 if you're ' carded', or you could be denied admission to nightclubs or forbidden to buy alcohol.

- Under-25s will find it hard to hire a car.

Time differences

- New York is on Eastern Standard Time: -5 hours from the UK, -6 hours from the rest of Europe.

Toilets (restrooms)

- Don't use public restrooms on the street, in stations or subways.
- Public buildings provide locked bathrooms (ask the doorman, cashier or receptionist for the key), or use those in hotel lobbies, bars or restaurants.

Electricity

- American current is 110–120 volts AC, so many European appliances need transformers as well as adapters. Wall outlets (socket points) take two-prong flat-pin plugs.

PUBLIC TRANSPORT

Subway

- New York's subway system has 469 stations, many open 24 hours (those with a green globe outside are always staffed).
- Since the recent major clean-up, cars are free of that famous dangerous-looking graffiti and are air-conditioned. Still, the system is confusing at first, and you will probably manage some mistakes.
- To ride the subway, you need a $1.25 token (get a 'Ten Pak' to save time, if not money) or a multiple-journey Metrocard. Drop the token or swipe the card to enter the turnstile; accompanying children under 44

inches tall ride free.

- Many stations have separate entrances for up- and downtown service, so ensure you're going the right way.
- Check that you are not about to get on a restricted-stop Express train that's going to whisk you to Brooklyn or the Bronx. Instead, take a 'Local' (a 'Brooklyn Bound Local' is a downtown-bound train making all stops).
- If you ride at night, stay in the 'Off Hour Waiting Area' until your train arrives, then use the middle cars.
- Transit information ☎ 718/330 1234 🕐 6AM–9PM

Bus

- Buses are safe, clean – and excruciatingly slow. The fastest are Limited Stop buses.
- Bus stops are on or near corners, marked by a sign and a yellow painted curb.
- Any length of ride costs the same as the subway, and you can use a token, a Metrocard, or the correct change, which you deposit on boarding, next to the driver. Ask the driver for a transfer which entitles you to a free onward or crosstown journey for an hour after boarding using the intersecting services listed on the back.
- A bus map showing many of the 200 routes travelled by the 3,700 blue and white buses is available from token booth clerks in subway stations, and is an essential accessory.

Taxis

- A yellow cab is available when the central number (not the 'Off Duty' side lights) on the roof is lit.
- All taxis display the current rates on the door, have a meter inside,

and can supply a printed receipt.
- Drivers are notorious for (a) knowing nothing about New York geography, (b) not speaking English and (c) having an improvisational driving style.
- Tip 15%. Bills larger than $10 are unpopular for short journeys.

MEDIA & COMMUNICATIONS

Telephones
- Public payphones are everywhere, and they nearly always work.
- Drop a 25¢ coin after lifting the receiver and before dialling to buy a 5-minute local call; an additional nickel or dime is requested at the end of that time.
- Most businesses have a toll-free 800 number, and practically all also have some version of touch-tone operated phone-answering computer, which is self-explanatory.
- To dial outside the 212 area, including 800 numbers, prefix the code with a '1'.
- Hotels can levy hefty surcharges, even on local calls, so use payphones instead.
- Prepaid phonecards were starting to become available at press time, and there are a few credit card phones.

Post offices
- The main post office (✉ Eighth Ave/33th St; ☎ 212/967 8585) is open 24 hours. Branch post offices are listed in the Yellow Pages (🕐 Mon–Fri 8–6, Sat 8–1).
- Stamps are also available from hotel concierges and vending machines in stores, for a 25% surcharge.
- Post letters in the blue metal mailboxes, or in the slots in office lobbies, air, train, and bus terminals, or at post offices.

Newspapers
- The local papers are the broadsheet *New York Times* (with a huge Sunday edition) and the tabloids: the *Daily News* and *New York Newsday*, both with generously supplemented Sunday editions, and the ailing *New York Post*. Also look for the respected *Wall Street Journal* and the pink-hued gossip-heavy *New York Observer*.

Magazines
- As well as the *New Yorker*, and *New York* (► 81), a New York edition of the London listings magazine, *Time Out*, was about to launch at press time. You may also see the self-consciously hip *The Paper*, and the free *Manhattan File*.

Radio
- Public funding for New York's excellent National Public Radio station WNYC, broadcasting classical and avant-garde music, jazz, news and cultural programming (on FM 93.9, and AM 820) was removed in 1995, but the station managed to survive by buying itself.
- New York, like most US cities, is the home of the 'shock jocks' of talk radio. The most famous is Howard Stern, who broadcasts Mon–Fri 6–10AM on FM 92.3 WXRK.

Television
- Hotels usually receive the 75 channels available to cable subscribers at last count. 'Main stream' TV includes the national networks and cable stations, the Public Broadcasting Service and the premium cable channels, such

as MTV, E and CNN.

- In addition there are bizarre Manhattan access channels, culture from the City University of New York (CUNY), New York 1 (with its constant onscreen weather update), plenty of home shopping as well as the live drama of Court TV.

International newsagents

- Many newsstands sell foreign newspapers; Hotalings (⊠ 142 W42nd St; ☎ 212/840 1868) is particularly well stocked.

EMERGENCIES

Lost property

- Be realistic – you are unlikely to recover something you lose. But try the following: Subway and bus ☎ 718/625 6200; Taxi ☎ 212/840 4734; JFK ☎ 718/656 4120; Newark ☎ 201/961 2230.

Medical treatment

- If you are unfortunate enough to need medical attention, you will be extremely thankful you took out adequate insurance. Any medical practitioner will ask for your insurance papers and/or a credit card or cash payment, and medical care is very expensive.
- In the event of an emergency, the 911 operator will send an ambulance. If you have more time in hand, you may opt for a private hospital rather than the overtaxed city-owned ones.
- The Doctors on Call service (☎ 212/737 2333) is 24-hour.
- Dental Emergency Service (☎ 212/679 3966, after 8 PM 212/679 4172).

Medicines

- Bring a prescription or doctor's certificate for any medications, in case of customs enquiries, as well as in the case of loss. Many drugs sold over the counter in Europe are prescription-only in the US.
- Pharmacies open 24 hours include Duane Reade (⊠ 485 Lexington Ave, 47th St; ☎ 212/682 5338, or 224 W57th St, Broadway; ☎ 212/541 9708).

Emergency phone numbers

- Police, Fire Department, Ambulance ☎ 911
- Crime Victims Hotline ☎ 212/577 7777
- Sex Crimes Report Line ☎ 212/267 7273
- Police, Fire Department, Ambulance for the deaf ☎ 800/342 4357

Consulates

- Australia ⊠ 636 Fifth Ave, ☎ 212/245 4000
- Canada ⊠ 1251 Sixth Ave, ☎ 212/586 2400
- Denmark ⊠ 825 Third Ave, ☎ 212/223 4545
- France ⊠ 934 Fifth Ave, ☎ 212/606 3600
- Germany ⊠ 460 Park Ave, ☎ 212/308 8700
- Ireland ⊠ 515 Madison Ave, ☎ 212/319 2555
- Italy ⊠ 690 Park Ave, ☎ 212/737 9100
- Netherlands ⊠ 1 Rockefeller Plaza, ☎ 212/249 1429
- Norway ⊠ 825 Third Ave, ☎ 212/421 7333
- Sweden ⊠ Dag Hammarskjøld Plaza, ☎ 212/751 5900
- UK ⊠ 845 Third Ave, ☎ 212/752 8400

TOURIST OFFICES

The New York Convention & Visitors' Bureau ⊠ 2 Columbus Circle ☎ 212/397 8222 ⓒ Mon–Fri 9–6; weekends 10–3

INDEX

ACKNOWLEDGEMENTS

The Automobile Association would like to thank the following photographers, picture libraries and associations for their help in the preparation of this book:
ALLSPORT UK LTD 47a (D Strohueyer), 47b (O Greule); THE FRICK COLLECTION 41b; THE MANSELL COLLECTION LTD 12; NEW YORK CONVENTION & VISITORS' BUREAU, INC 60; REX FEATURES LTD 9; E ROONEY 59

The remaining pictures are held in the Association's own library (AA PHOTO LIBRARY) with contributions from: D CORRANCE 2, 6, 13a, 15, 16, 19, 21, 27b, 29a, 30, 33b, 35a, 40, 44a, 44b, 51, 52, 53; R G ELLIOTT 1, 5b, 17, 20, 24a, 26, 27a, 28, 32, 34, 35b, 37a, 38a, 41a, 42, 43a, 43b, 45, 46, 49a, 55, 61b, 87a; P KENWARD 5a, 7, 13b, 18, 23a, 23b, 24b, 25, 29b, 31a, 31b, 33a, 36, 37b, 38b, 39, 48, 49b, 50, 56, 57, 58, 61a, 87b.

Copy-editor: *Karin Fancett*
Verifier: *Joanna Whitaker*
Indexer: *Marie Lorimer*
Original design: *Design FX*